Arms and Industry

A Study of the Foundations of International Polity

By

Norman Angell

Author of "The Great Illusion," etc.

G. P. Putnam's Sons
New York and London
The Knickerbocker Press
1914

The Knickerbocker Press, New York

PREFACE TO AMERICAN EDITION

It is an integral part of the arguments here presented that certain underlying problems of organized society—with which this book attempts to deal—concern Americans as deeply as they concern any of the other groups composing that society. For I have attempted here to show that the civilized world has become, not merely economically, but morally and intellectually, interdependent. If the price of money in Europe, and the credit conditions generally there, concern in a very vital and concrete fashion American capitalists and workmen who may have no visible relation with Europe at all, so equally is the social reformer concerned with the direction which may be given by the drift of European politics to European thought, a fact very visibly illustrated of course in such matters as Socialism, Syndicalism, class war, the relations of the sexes, religion. Never in written history has any considerable intellectual fermentation been set up in one group without ultimately affecting all. Less than ever to-day can such fermentation take account of frontiers. American society as much as any will be affected by the operations throughout the world of the forces here dealt with.

Preface to American Edition

Although the six chapters of this book appear in the form of various addresses delivered to audiences having apparently as little in common as those at the British Association and a group of German universities, the Institute of Bankers of Great Britain and the Royal United Service Institution of that country, the papers have been so selected as to represent the natural development and elaboration of an underlying general principle and to make a connected whole. I have attempted to render this unity still plainer by summarizing the entire argument in an introductory chapter of some length.

As each paper was in its original form an independent production, there is necessarily some slight repetition of argument and illustration. I have been at no special pains to correct this. It is a somewhat transparent literary convention that a reader, in following an argument through several hundred pages, will always recall in the latter part the precise details of a fact or illustration given in an earlier part, or will refer thereto; and that on no account should such fact or illustration be repeated. I have deemed it a service to the reader and an economy of his attention to disregard this convention in one or two cases.

I am indebted to the editors of the *Journal of the Royal United Service Institution* and the *Journal of the Institute of Bankers* for permission to reprint addresses which have appeared in their publications, and to Messrs. Watts and Co. of London for permission to reprint a portion of the Conway Memorial address delivered at South Place Institute.

I am glad to take this opportunity of acknowledging my very deep sense of gratitude and indebtedness to more friends than I can mention, in England, Germany, France, and America, who, since the appearance of an earlier work of mine in 1910, have helped me with suggestions, advice, and criticism. To certain friends in the universities of those countries I am in a special sense indebted, notably, in America, to Presidents Nicholas Murray Butler of Columbia and David Starr Jordan of Stanford. Dr. George W. Nasmyth has rendered invaluable assistance in the revision of proof. As to the larger number who in England, Germany, and America during that period have made great personal sacrifices to encourage and organize in a definite way the study of the subjects dealt with here, it would be impertinent and fatuous in an author to assume that thanks are due from him. I happen to know how great in many cases those sacrifices have been, but they have been made on behalf of a general cause of intellectual sanitation to which my own works are, happily, but a small contribution.

NORMAN ANGELL.

LONDON,
January, 1914.

CONTENTS

INTRODUCTORY SUMMARY OF ARGUMENT

THE argument developed in this book attempts to show that the political ideas which at present shape the conduct and determine the attitude of one State to another in Europe, and give to international relationship its present character, are erroneous, despite their general acceptance as self-evident and axiomatic; that they are the outcome of certain abstract theories at variance with the facts.

This does not necessarily imply that the statesmen who pursue a particular policy, or the public who endorse it, do so because they have well-defined principles of action based upon clearly-conceived theorems. But their action is nevertheless the result of certain general ideas as to what is to the advantage of their country, and as to the means by which that advantage can be secured; and it is the supremacy of such ideas that creates the present condition of international society, just as it is the prevailing ideas among the units which compose any society, whether that of a cannibal island or a Catholic nunnery, which determine its character. The story of civilization is the story of the development of ideas: the Palæolithic man of Northern Europe was physically a much finer man than the modern Londoner, as is, indeed, the present-day Cameroon cannibal. The qualities which explain the differences between their respective social states are intellectual and moral.

The fundamental ideas to which we must go for any comprehensive explanation of international politics are also, of course, those which lie at the base of political behaviour within the nation, though in this case they are modified by influences which do not operate in the case of relations between separate communities. But it is precisely because the conceptions here dealt with concern in some degree all forms of political action that their study has a range of practical interest much wider than that of the problems embodied in the term "international politics." For not only do current misconceptions prompt in the international field political action which by universal consent defeats the end which it is intended to promote (such as the safety and material and moral well-being of the respective nations), and produces such visible evils as war and armaments, but the misconceptions also give rise to less visible but more profound evils in the internal structure of nations, in the forms of government, the methods of administration, the means employed to achieve social ends, the direction of political ideals and emotions, the nature of the defined ideas and the undefined instincts that affect deeply the character of men's relations to each other and to nature, and affect in consequence their moral quality generally.

The scope of the present book, however, is limited to showing the nature of the misconceptions in so far as international action is concerned, and only so far as it may be necessary for that purpose to make clear their philosophical foundation is their wider bearing touched upon.

What are the tenets of that diplomatic orthodoxy here challenged? In order to render the issue clear, I have summarized their best expression as one may find it, not merely in the works of those special authorities on diplomacy and polity, of which Machiavelli was the prototype, but in the declarations of European statesmen and public men, dealing with actual problems, in current journalism of the better sort, and generally in that part of the discussion of the subject most likely to represent public opinion and affect policy. In England, France, Germany, or America, any such discussion of international problems would imply conceptions which include the following assumptions:

"The fact that each nation is a sovereign independent entity involves the further fact that each is dependent for the protection of its rights and interests against the attacks of others upon its own force. The relinquishment of the use of force by any one State would be equivalent to acquiescence in possible wrong; should a stronger State take against ourselves or others an action which we believe wrong, we should have no means of supporting the right as against it. And as, presumably, that State least likely to be right would be the most likely to use force, the attempt to vindicate morality by refusing to use force would be to defeat the aim which prompted such a policy.

"The fact that each unit in the 'Society' of nations is an independent entity of increasing needs and population in a world of limited space and opportunity involves the further fact that each must compete with the rest for sustenance and as that implies, for life itself. There may not be direct preying one upon the other, but the pre-emption of space and opportunity by the strong means the exclusion (which is equivalent to the destruction) of the weak, so that the efficiency of one nation in its occupation or exploitation of the earth involves, with however little intention or desire, the loss and damage, potential or actual, of another, a condition which has its parallel in the economic competition of individuals, by which the capacity and energy of one trader or manufacturer means suffering to the workpeople and dependents of a less capable rival. This situation is illustrated very visibly by such incidents of the Protectionist System (supported by some of the most humane and civilized nations of the world) as that by which the promotion of industry in one country creates areas of starvation in another, and by such incidents of modern policy as that by which the surplus population of an overcrowded country like India is excluded from a relatively empty country like Australia. These economic, social, and political phenomena, accepted as inevitable incidents of human struggle, reconcile us to a conception of international society in which the units are, because sovereign and independent, either passively and indirectly, or actively and directly, rival and predatory. The survival of any given unit depends in the last resort upon the relative degree of physical force which it is able to exercise against competitors, whereby to impose its own or resist another's exploitation of the earth, just as on the moral side force is necessary to impose our view of right as against a hostile view if we are unwilling to acquiesce in what we believe to be wrong.

"In other words, an international society, in the sense of a society such as exists within the frontiers of civilized States, does not exist and cannot, so long as nations are sovereign and independent. For, in the case of communities within the respective States, society exists by virtue of the surrender of some part of the independence and sovereignty of the unit—the individual—to the sovereignty of the State, which exercises physical force for the purpose of establishing the common will in the shape of law, restraining thus the predatory instincts of the units. But the society of nations possesses no corresponding supreme sanction and sovereignty. Moreover, that degree of unity in aim and in social and moral ideas which alone in the case of national communities renders possible a common sanction and sovereignty does not exist at present as between separate nations; indeed, the fact of their separate existence is due precisely to the absence of such unity and to the desire for independence—a desire which has been accentuated in recent years, as witness the intensification of 'Nationality' and the determination of the younger communities to protect themselves from alien, and especially Asiatic, admixture. The surrender, therefore, of national independence and sovereignty to any degree corresponding to the surrender of independence which takes place in the case of citizens of the same State, is a price much higher than that which the progressive nations of the world are prepared to pay for the purpose of securing a cosmopolitan State exercising that supreme sanction of physical force which is the necessary basis of any real society. If the alternative is between two orders—one in which each struggles for the preservation of its distinctive national ideals and life, and the advantages that go with the successful imposition of its strength; and the other in which, for the purpose of being relieved of the risks and costs of struggle, it surrenders in favour of a more cosmopolitan ideal, in some degree, its distinctive and special social values and, entirely, the advantages given by its power over others—it is certain that the stronger nations will choose the former alternative. Materially and morally they will deem the risks of competition and struggle to be preferable to the security which would come of a common pooling and distribution by consent. To the weak only would such appeal. The strong will naturally prefer to see as much international law and civilized intercourse as may be between nations maintained, as now, by virtue of an equilibrium of forces sufficiently stable to insure that it will not be disturbed save on vital issues—always, however, in danger of such disturbance, owing to the fact that a preponderance of force on the part of one unit can be used in relation to the rest to tilt the balance of advantage in its favour, the central fact which necessarily makes the whole system one in which physical force is the ultimate appeal, the one condition of survival economically, socially, and morally."

The object of the six papers of which this book is composed is to show, step by step, that this theory ignores the facts or is based upon a demonstrable misreading of them.

Save only in a narrow juridical sense, which, as will be indicated, does not affect the vital functions of society, the nations which form the European community are not sovereign, nor independent, nor entities, nor rival, nor advantageously predatory; nor does the exercise or possession of the means of physical coercion determine the relative advantage of each; nor is physical coercion within their borders the ultimate sanction of social organization, of law and justice. Military power is irrelevant to the promotion of the aims, moral and material, postulated in that statement of political principles which I have just given.

To realize how deep-set is the fallacy involved therein, it is necessary to have in mind something of the process by which mankind maintains its life and increases its numbers in the world—for it is the only species of living thing which by its own efforts permanently increases its relative place in nature, the only one which by its own efforts directly affects the means of subsistence available for it. For birds or beasts or fishes, the quantity of food available in Nature is a fixed quantity unaffected by their efforts. The birds do not breed and protect earth-worms, the rabbits do not cultivate plants.* The efforts of the individual

* I am aware, of course, that there are rudimentary forms of

are therefore limited to assuring for itself the largest possible share of the fixed quantity available for the species. In such conditions, success of one individual may mean deprivation for another. Struggle between them (though, incidentally, it seldom takes the form of members of the same species preying directly upon one another) is a necessary condition of survival. But man has increased his means of subsistence and his chances of survival by conscious adjustment of the forces of Nature, by directing forces, that would otherwise destroy him, to his own ends. He repels one force, the rain or snow or cold, by using others—trees for houses, coal for fuel. He thus turns Nature against herself. But he can only do this thanks to one fact—that he is, by his intelligence, able to create a union of forces by co-operating with his fellows. If men acted as isolated units, this effective fight against the forces of Nature would not be possible. The condition of man would be that of any other animal that neither grows its food nor makes its clothes nor warms its dwelling.* But as soon as this union takes place, the co-operation of other members of his species becomes of more value to him than their disappearance or destruction. Indeed, as these pages show, the process of co-operation rapidly creates a condition in which, if one of two parties is to survive, both must survive; if one

co-operation among animals, but the contrast is more than sufficiently true for illustration.

* See pp. 16–22 seq.

perishes, both perish.* Thus a small but feebly co-operating population (like the Indian tribes of North America) had less of subsistence than a population many hundred times as great occupying the same space, and having only the same natural sources available, but having a much more highly developed capacity for co-operation.†

Now, the governing method of co-operation must be division of labour, and that method necessarily implies interdependence between those party to it; the mechanical forces which are necessarily created by a condition of interdependence progressively nullify the effectiveness of physical coercion employed by either party against the other. To the extent to which a party possessing means of physical force has need of the party against which he exercises them, they tend to become ineffective. If the dependence is merely of a simple and partial kind, like that of a slave owner upon slaves that he can readily replace, and of whom he demands merely physical exertion, the operation of physical compulsion may be effective for his relatively simple purpose. He can, if he has been more intelligent than they in organizing means of protection, kill them if they refuse to work. But if the dependence is more complete, so that an absolutely essential labour is done by slaves who cannot be replaced, he cannot kill them and his force is limited; if the labour is of a complex kind demanding wide intelligence, like scientific

* See p. 18 seq. † See pp. 156–157 seq.

research, or elaborate organization and administration, the effectiveness of physical force declines by reason of another order of factors, until, as the complexity and interdependence increase, the element of physical force disappears and the sanction of physical compulsion is gradually replaced by another.*

Now, these two factors—the need for widespread co-operation to find our sustenance, and the decline in the effectiveness of physical force as a means of securing services in a co-operative process of any complexity—have done two things: they have destroyed not merely the economic, but the moral and intellectual unity and homogeneity of States; and they have rendered the exercise of force by one State against another, for economic, moral, or intellectual purposes, futile, because ineffective and irrelevant to the end in view.†

Co-operation between nations has become essential for the very life of their peoples.‡ But that co-operation does not take place as between States at all. A trading corporation "Britain" does not buy cotton from another corporation "America." A manufacturer in Manchester strikes a bargain with a merchant in Louisiana in order to keep a bargain with a dyer in Germany, and three or a much larger number of parties enter into virtual, or perhaps actual, contract, and form a mutually dependent economic community (numbering, it may be, with the work people in the

* See pp. 106–110 seq. † See pp. 163–169 seq.
‡ See pp. 115–119; 166 seq.

group of industries involved, some millions of individuals)—an economic entity so far as one can exist which does not include all organized society. The special interests of such a community may become hostile to those of another community, but it will almost certainly not be a "national" one, but one of a like nature, say a shipping ring or groups of international bankers or Stock Exchange speculators. The frontiers of such communities do not coincide with the areas in which operate the functions of the State. How could a State, say Britain, act on behalf of an economic entity such as that just indicated? By pressure against America or Germany? But the community against which the British manufacturer in this case wants pressure exercised is not "America" or "Germany"—both Americans and Germans are his partners in the matter. He wants it exercised against the shipping ring or the speculators or the bankers who in part are British. If Britain injures America and Germany as a whole, she injures necessarily the economic entity which it was her object to protect.*

This establishes two things, therefore: the fact that the political and economic units do not coincide, and the fact which follows as a consequence: that action by political authorities designed to control economic activities which take no account of the limits of political jurisdiction is necessarily irrelevant and ineffective. The assumption that

*See pp. 22–24 and 100–105 seq.

States are economically rival, and that economic advantage accrues to the possession of political power based on military force, postulates communities capable of political and geographical limitation that are self-contained, and postulates also the effective control of the social and economic activities of similar other communities by the military force of our own. The great nations of modern Europe have passed out of that stage of development in which such a conception bears even a distant relation to the facts. This condition carries with it the intangibility of wealth so far as foreign State action is concerned, because any State destroying wealth in another must destroy wealth in its own, since the unit intersects the two areas.*

On the economic side this development is relatively modern—its vital form belongs to our generation.† The prime factor therein has, of course, been the improvement of communication and the cheapening of transport, setting up a division of labour, with its consequent interdependence and solidarity of interest, between groups situated in different nations thus rendering hostility based on the lines of political geography irrelevant to real collision of interest and moral conflict. It is by the fact of having set up this process, and not by the fact of having brought people of different nations into touch, that improved communication is transforming the character of international

* See pp. 22–24 and 100–105 seq. † See pp. 108–130 seq.

relations. People do not necessarily become less hostile by virtue of "knowing one another better," and seeing much of one another, or we should have had no wars of religion, or the bitter racial, religious, political, economic, and social conflicts that exist in communities the members of which see each other every day. The negro conflict in America, anti-Semitism in Russia, the racial conflicts of South-Eastern Europe, the perpetual revolutions of Spanish America, are but a few of numberless cases illustrating the point.

What concerns us here is that, even in those conflicts in which physical force might conceivably play some rôle, it is irrelevant when exercised by States, because the State lines do not follow the lines of the respective conflicts, and because moral possessions cannot be protected by force; these only become secure by virtue of a general agreement not to resort to force, and a general recognition of the truth of this must precede any hope of securing the agreement—which in the most vital cases is not a formal agreement at all, but an implied one.

That intersection of the political by the economic boundaries just described has a close moral and intellectual parallel. The nation which should use its military power to arrest or destroy the intellectual or moral conception of some other nation—a religious, political, or social belief—would certainly be entering into war against an identical belief held by groups within its own community. And, again, just as the economic and commercial activities of the world are not carried on by Governments acting as corporations, but by the individuals within different States setting up activities that operate across the political divisions, in the same way it is not the Governments that think and modify opinion, but the individuals acting in conscious or unconscious co-operation with individuals in foreign and "rival" States. The great movements of all time, even long before improved communications had made of Europe a single intellectual organism, have been the joint work of men of many nations. The religious Reformation, the French Revolution and all that arose therefrom, are modern cases which have had their parallel in all written history. And just as the physical life of a large proportion of the British population is only rendered possible because in their economic activities they act as dependent parts of a larger whole, so it is only by virtue of forming a part of a larger moral and intellectual whole that it has acquired those attributes which we deem characteristic of the British—such as representative political institutions—all based upon a general knowledge made possible by such foreign importations, its alphabet, its mathematics, printing, its Christian religion, both of the older and newer form, its newer political and social movements—all the result of intellectual co-operation with a larger than a purely national world.*

* See pp. 30–35; 57–60 seq.

The arbitrary assertion that, even cut off from European and Eastern society, "Britain" would have developed this knowledge and these arts and moralities is, of course, capable neither of proof nor disproof. All we can say is, that that is not the way she has acquired them.

How irrelevant are conflicts based on State boundaries to the deeper divisions is illustrated by the relation of the Western and Christian, to the Eastern and non-Christian world. This is supposed to be one of the most vital of the issues, from which no egress can be found save by the military action of States. Yet, within the lifetime of men still living, we have seen the armies of two Western and Christian Powers allied with an Eastern and Mohammedan against a third Christian Power; we have seen the policy of the British Empire committed for nearly two generations to an attempt to strengthen a retrograde Asiatic Power against the Christian and more progressive forces that surrounded her. The habit of thinking in States leads Englishmen to the conclusion that they have no particular interest in the defence of Pennsylvania or Massachusetts, or any other American State, and all that their civilization represents in the way of future outlets for our children and as a bulwark of Western culture, but that it is worth while giving immensely of blood and treasure for the defence of Burma or the Deccan; the same habit leads Germans to the conclusion (in the British view) that it is to their best interest to diminish British influence and increase Turkish and Japanese; it leads Frenchmen to the conclusion that Western culture can best be promoted by the support of Russia as against Germany. And so on and so on. It is in this way that the maintenance of the military power of States and the older conception of human divisions works for the defence of the higher culture against the lower!

But in order more fully to realize the true relation of force to the protection of the moral possessions of separate communities, it is necessary to realize the true nature of that relation within the community. An immense confusion exists here because the defective terminology of the science of society leads us to use the same word for two opposed processes. The basis of social security is not physical coercion, it is the cancellation of coercion by an equivalent counterbalancing force.

The one unquestionably useful work of political organization of government has been the elimination of coercion as between men—the work of assuring in some degree at least that one citizen does not use physical coercion against another. Its function is to prevent the use of force; it does that by cancelling it. If the robber attempts the use of force, the force of the government (through the policeman, for instance) is thrown against him and his force is cancelled. In the case of an honest difference between two citizens, it is not the preponderance of physical weight which determines the issue between them, but the combined intelligence of the community, as we have it expressed in law (I am giving the theory of the thing, of course), deciding which settlement will best make for the efficient co-operation of the community.

Not even the most stupid pretend that the method in all its details, or in all cases, works to perfection. But it is an improvement on the older method of each man using his force against his fellows, a method which mankind had to abandon as soon as, and to the degree to which, it had need of social co-operation at all. Improvement will come, not by reversion to the old method, but by the development of the new. Where government confines its exercise of physical force to the cancellation of the coercion of one citizen by another, leaving intelligence free to fix the several adjustments either through extra-juridical means or through the improvement of law, there is possibility of improving such adjustments. Only when government itself becomes a user of force, not for the purpose of the cancellation of coercion, but in the positive sense, basing the imposition of its will, not upon agreement, but upon the mere possession of power to impose it, and abandoning or suppressing the effort through discussion to establish the common will—then only does possibility of improvement stop.

Government in Western nations is now universally based, ostensibly at least, upon the policy just indicated; it is assumed to represent, not the mere accidental possession of force, but the common will and interest. Where political privilege exists—not by virtue of the utility of the function which those who enjoy that privilege perform, but merely by virtue of the fact that they hold means of coercion as against those upon whom it is imposed—this arrangement is deemed to fall short of Western ideals. The internal polity of the higher type of Western nation is based upon the acceptance of a convention by which the use of force shall be withheld. The British Government does not hold its office by virtue of the physical force which it exercises, because in that case it would not withdraw upon an adverse vote of the people, but use the army (which it commands) to retain its power and would only be dislodged when another army—that of a revolution—was brought against it. Where force is the ultimate sanction, as it is in certain military civilizations like some in South America, the conflict is one of military power. But in the civilist polity of more orderly States the sanction is the general will of the community expressed through Parliamentary institutions or otherwise. Nor is it the fact that in order to secure collective action there must be the implied threat of coercion; collective action can equally be secured by the agreement of those who do not approve a given line of action to acquiesce on condition that they shall be free to persuade, if they can, other parties to the compact to modify it. Conservatives acquiesce in Liberal legislation on the understanding that they shall alter it if they can win the country over to their view. The whole arrangement is based on the implied agreement that neither party should take advantage of its possession of the instruments of coercion to use them against the other. When this agreement is not observed, there is a movement away from the British towards the Venezuelan or Turkish type of society. The basis of British society is the observation of the convention not to use force.

This polity, which is the basis of organized society as between rival communities within modern States, is not yet *recognized* as operative between the political bodies which we call nations save with reference to one group—the nations of the British Empire. We have therein a community of five independent States between whom arise at times very serious differences (as between Natal and India, and Britain and Australia), and in their case we have formal recognition of the convention that coercion shall not be used by one as against the other, a convention easier to maintain than in the case of parties in the same state, because there is no real need of common political action between them.

It was very generally recognized in Britain recently that the difficulties which arose as between India and Natal were very grave indeed. Had Great Britain in that case been dealing with a foreign Power, the question of a *casus belli* would certainly have arisen (Lord Hardinge's speech made that plain). But British public men and the British Press alike agreed that, however wrong the attitude of Natal might be, the fact that she was a self-governing colony precluded the possibility of Britain's using compulsion in the matter. But while this principle has only received formal recognition in the case of the States of the British Empire, in practice it is much more widely operative. Britons, like the people of many of the older nations, have sunk thousands of millions in foreign investments, the real security of which is not any physical force which their Government could possibly exercise, but the free recognition of foreigners that it is to their advantage to adhere to financial obligations. Britons do not even pretend that the security of their investments in a country like America, or even Argentina, is dependent upon the coercion which the British Government is able to exercise over those countries.* And not merely do they trust their money, but their lives, to the protection of a like order of moral force. The physical force of Great Britain could not certainly ever be effectively

* I happened to have learned a year or two since that a British politician, whose public utterances at the time of the German invasion scare included one to the effect that "the only secure protection against the cupidity of Germanic hordes was an overwhelming British fleet," was himself the owner of German industrial debentures, had sent a son to be educated in Germany, and was accustomed to go to a German watering-place, where he placed himself in the hands of German doctors!

operative in Switzerland or Austria, yet every summer tens of thousands of Britons trust their lives and those of their womenkind and children to no better security than the expectation that a foreign community over whom we have no possibility of exercising force will observe a convention which has no sanction other than the recognition that it is to their advantage to observe it. And we thus have the spectacle of millions of Britons absolutely convinced that the sanctity of their homes and the safety of their property are secure from the ravages of the foreigner only because they possess a naval and military force that overawes him, yet serenely leaving the protection of that military force, and placing life and property alike within the absolute power of that very foreigner against whose predatory tendencies we spend millions in protecting ourselves.

No use of military power, however complete and overwhelming, would pretend to afford a protection anything like as complete as that afforded by these moral forces. Sixty years ago Britain had as against Greece a preponderance of power that made her the absolute dictator of the latter's policy yet all the British battleships and all the threats of "consequences" could not prevent British travellers being murdered by Greek brigands, though in Switzerland only moral forces—the recognition by an astute people of the advantage of treating foreigners well—had already made the lives and property of Britons as safe in that country as in their own.

In the same way, no scheme of arming Protestants as against Catholics, or Catholics as against Protestants (the method which gave us the wars of religion and massacre of St. Bartholomew), or of Conservatives as against Liberals (which gives us San Domingo and Venezuela), could assure that general security of spiritual and intellectual possessions which we now in large measure enjoy.

We have seen how strong and effective are those social forces just sketched in assuring men security, and how feeble, irrelevant, and finally self-stultifying, in achieving the same ends is military force. We have seen also that Europeans in their individual conduct recognize this and give their practical allegiance to the first method, and that by so doing they help to develop it, and yet in their political conduct, in the policies of their Governments, still adhere to the second method and disparage the first; that all their political effort, energy, and emotion are based upon theories and principles which all their daily and private conduct flouts.

How comes this contradiction?

It is, in part at least, because men give to the management of their own affairs, in the development of their business, in the investment of their money, the education of their children, a care and thoroughness of attention which they do not give (and cannot be expected to give) to politics, which are so largely other people's affairs. The first is the outcome of specialized knowledge, the training of a lifetime; the second is not.* And judgments based on rapid superficial views will be influenced mainly by the visible and tangible, to the disregard of the invisible and intangible but none the less real. Armies and navies are visible and tangible things; "social forces" are not; the sovereignty of a State embodied in a King or Cabinet is visible; the World State, though real, is intangible; a sanction expressed in a printed law is visible; the sanction of mutual dependence, compelling far more powerfully it may be than could law the observance of a compact, is invisible; a "possession" in the shape of a colony can be seen on the map, though the only proprietary rights we have therein may be much less numerous than our proprietary rights in countries that are marked on maps as "rivals."

And the weight of an unexamined and obsolete political terminology is, though more subtle, probably just as powerful. The Professor of a great University, a teacher of history, and a student of constitutional law, once thought to score a point by asking: "Were those who believed that possession of extended territory did not enrich a people prepared to see Great Britain give away Canada?" He was asked how he supposed

* This fact was remarked once by the late Lord Salisbury in reply to a delegation of City men. He said, "You act as politicians as you would never act as business men," and hinted pretty plainly that their political conduct was guided by a superficiality of view that they would never allow to control their commercial conduct.

Great Britain could "give away" the inhabitants of Canada, and what proprietary right she possessed in those eight million human beings?

Both the phrases and the pictures which they imply are, of course, an historical survival from a time when a colonial "plantation" was really somebody's possession (the monopoly of some company of trading adventurers or a Court favourite); or from a still earlier time when political "ownership" was a quite real thing from the point of view of some reigning family to whom a country was an estate; or from the period in Europe when the trade of "government" was as much the professional interest of an oligarchic group as banking or cotton-spinning are definite industrial interests of our day.

We have here, then, two factors: the general currency of words and pictures that were created to indicate conditions that have passed away, and the interpretation of these words and pictures by people compelled by the inevitable circumstances of their lives to form their political conceptions hurriedly and superficially—from the newspaper headline, the vague chatter of smoking-room leisure. Now to these add another factor—one which the pro-military critic seems to imagine the civilist overlooks, though it is in reality the basis of the whole case, the most important fact in all this discussion—namely, that the element in man which makes him capable, however feebly, of choice in the matter of conduct, the one fact distinguishing him from that vast multitude of living things which act unreflectingly, instinctively (in the proper and scientific sense of the word), as the mere physical reaction to external prompting, is something not deeply rooted, since it is the latest addition of all to our nature. The really deeply-rooted motives of conduct, those having by far the greatest biological momentum, are naturally the "motives" of the plant and the animal, the kind that marks in the main the acts of all living things save man, the unreflecting motives, those containing no element of ratiocination and free volition, that almost mechanical reaction to external forces which draw the leaves towards the sun rays and makes the tiger tear its living food limb from limb.

To make plain what that really means in human conduct, we must recall the character of that process by which man turns the forces of Nature to his service instead of allowing them to overwhelm him. We saw that its essence was a union of individual forces against the common enemy, the forces of Nature. Where men in isolated action would have been powerless, and would have been destroyed, union, association, co-operation, enabled them to survive. Survival was contingent upon the cessation of struggle between them, and the substitution therefor of common action. Now, the process both in the beginning and in the subsequent development of this device of co-operation is important. It was born of a failure of force.

If the isolated force had sufficed, the union of force would not have been resorted to. But such union is not a mere mechanical multiplication of blind energies: it is a combination involving will, intelligence. If mere multiplication of physical energy had determined the result of man's struggles he would have been destroyed or be the helpless slave of the animals of which he makes his food.* He has overcome them as he has overcome the flood and the storm—by quite another order of action. Intelligence only emerges where physical force is ineffective.

I have already in this summary touched upon, and in the pages that follow more fully described† the almost mechanical process by which, as the complexity of co-operation grows, the element of physical compulsion declines in effectiveness, and is replaced by agreement based on mutual recognition of advantage. There is through every step of the development the same phenomenon: intelligence and agreement only emerge as force becomes ineffective. In human relations it generally becomes ineffective through resistance. The early (and purely illustrative) slave owner who spent his days seeing that his slave did not run away, and compelling him to work, realized the economic defect of the arrangement; most of the effort,

* It is a curious fact, by the way, that the physically great monsters—the dinosaurus, the plesiosaurus, the labyrinthodon, the mastodon—have disappeared in favour of much smaller animals.

† See pp. 18–20; 106–110 seq.

physical and intellectual, of the slave was devoted to trying to escape; that of the owner, trying to prevent him. The force of the one, intellectual or physical, cancelled the force of the other, and the energies of both were lost so far as productive value was concerned, and the needed task, the building of the shelter or the catching of the fish, was not done or badly done, and both went short as to food and shelter. But from the moment that they struck a bargain as to the division of labour and of spoils, and adhered to it, the full energies of both were liberated for direct production, and the economic effectiveness of the arrangement was not merely doubled, but probably multiplied many times. But this substitution of free agreement for coercion, with all that it implied of contract, of "what is fair," and all that followed of mutual reliance in the fulfilment of the agreement, was *based upon mutual recognition of advantage.* Now, that recognition, without which the arrangement could not exist at all, required, relatively, a considerable mental effort, *due in the first instance to the failure of force.* If the slave owner had had more effective means of physical coercion, and had been able to subdue his slave, he would not have bothered about agreement, and this embryo of human society and justice would not have been brought into being. And in history its development has never been constant, but marked by the same rise and fall of the two orders of motive: as soon as one party or the other obtained such preponderance of strength as promised to be effective, he showed a tendency to drop free agreement and use force; this, of course, immediately provoked the resistance of the other, with a lesser or greater reversion to the earlier profitless condition.

This perpetual tendency to abandon the social arrangement and resort to physical coercion is, of course, easily explainable by the biological fact just touched on. To realize at each turn and permutation of the division of labour that the social arrangement was, after all, the best, demanded on the part of the two characters in our sketch, not merely control of instinctive actions, but a relatively large ratiocinative effort for which the biological history of early man had not fitted him. The physical act of compulsion only required a stone axe and a quickness of purely physical movement for which his biological history had afforded infinitely long training. The more mentally-motived action, that of social conduct, demanding reflection as to its effect on others, and the effect of that reaction upon our own position and a conscious control of physical acts, is of modern growth; it is but skin-deep; its biological momentum is feeble. Yet on that feeble structure has been built all civilisation.

When we remember this—how frail are the ultimate foundations of our fortress, how much those spiritual elements which alone can give us human society are outnumbered by the prehuman elements—is it surprising that those pre-social promptings of which civilization represents the conquest occasionally overwhelm man, break up the solidarity of his army, and push him back a stage or two nearer to the brute condition from which he came; that even at this moment he is groping blindly as to the method of distributing in the order of his most vital needs the wealth he is able to wring from the earth; that some of his most fundamental social and political conceptions —those, among others, with which we are now dealing—have little relation to real facts; that his animosities and hatreds are as purposeless and meaningless as his enthusiasms and his sacrifices; that emotion and effort which quantitatively would suffice amply for the greater tasks before him, for the firmer establishment of justice and well-being, for the cleaning up of all the festering areas of moral savagery that remain, are as a simple matter of fact turned to those purposes hardly at all, but to objects which, to the degree to which they succeed, merely stultify each other?

Now, this fact, the fact that civilization is but skin-deep and that man is so largely the unreflecting brute, is not denied by pro-military critics of civilist philosophy. On the contrary, they appeal to it as the first and last justification of their policy. "All your talk will never get over human nature; men are not guided by logic; passion is bound to get the upper hand," and such phrases, are a sort of Greek chorus supplied by the military party to the whole of this discussion.

Nor do the militarist advocates deny that these unreflecting elements are anti-social; again, it is part of their case that, unless they are held in check by the "iron hand," they will submerge society in a welter of savagery. Nor do they deny—it is hardly possible to do so—that the most important securities which we enjoy, the possibility of living in mutual respect of right because we have achieved some understanding of right; all that distinguishes modern Europe from the Europe of (among other things) religious wars and St. Bartholomew massacres, and distinguishes British political methods from those of Turkey or Venezuela, are due to the development of moral forces (since physical force is most resorted to in the less desirable age and area), and particularly to the general recognition that you cannot solve religious and political problems by submitting them to the irrelevant hazard of physical force.

We have got thus far, then: both parties to the discussion are agreed as to the fundamental fact that civilization is based upon moral and intellectual elements in constant danger of being overwhelmed by more deeply-rooted anti-social elements. The plain facts of history past and present are there to show that where those moral elements are absent the mere fact of the possession of arms only adds to the destructiveness of the resulting welter.

The civilist party says:

"As the first and last factors of civilization are the moral and intellectual capacities of its units, our first efforts must centre upon their protection and development. They will, obviously, have best chance of survival if we can eliminate as far as possible the chances of physical collision, just as they have been eliminated in the religious field and in the field of internal politics among Western nations, and if we can eliminate the destructiveness of each of the opposing forces in case we should yield to our unseeing passions."

The militarist party says:

"'Men are savage, blood-thirsty creatures who, when their blood is up, will fight for nothing, for a word, for a sign.'* We should therefore disparage the development of all counteracting intellectual and moral forces, and take every precaution to see that their capacity for damage when in that condition of blind excitement is . . . as great as possible. All else is chimera and useless theorizing."

I have certainly no intention of doing any injustice to militarist advocacy in this last conclusion, and none is done, for the whole attitude of such advocacy is literally and exactly what I have indicated. All attempts to secure our safety by other than military means are not merely regarded with indifference: they are more generally treated either with a truly ferocious contempt or with definite condemnation.

This apparently on two grounds: first, that

* *Spectator.*

nothing that we can do will affect the conduct of other nations; secondly, that, in the development of those moral forces which do undoubtedly give us security, government action—which political effort has in view—can play no part.

Both assumptions are, of course, groundless. The first implies not only that our own conduct and our own ideas need no examination, but that ideas current in one country have no reaction on those of another, and that the political action of one State does not affect that of others. The second means, in reality, that nothing can be done because nothing has been done. In these pages* and elsewhere† I have shown how immensely political action can be made to develop those social and moral forces here dealt with, and how the individual action of one State can be made to react upon that of others. But such a fact is not realized because the feebly-developed social instinct which military philosophy implies not merely disregards the immense weight of the social forces at work, but inhibits any effective conception of the fact that the value of a policy must be judged by its effect when adopted by all parties. "The way to be sure of peace is to be so much stronger than your enemy that he will not dare to attack you,"‡ is the type

* See pp. 185–202.

† See "The Great Illusion," Part III. (Heinemann, London) and "War and the Workers," Chapter V. (National Labour Press, Manchester).

‡ Mr. Winston Churchill.

of accepted and much-applauded "axioms," the unfortunate corollary of which is (since both parties can adopt the rule) that peace will only be finally achieved when each is stronger than the other.

So thought and acted the man with the stone axe in our illustration, and in both cases the psychological motive is the same: the long-inherited impulse to isolated action, to the solution of a difficulty by some simple form of physical movement; the tendency to break through the more lately acquired habit of action based on social compact and on the mental realization of its advantage. It is the reaction against intellectual effort and responsible control of instinct, a form of natural protest very common in children and in adults not brought under the influence of social discipline.

Incidentally the conception that the only possible social relationship is for one party to be in a position to impose its will and for the other to accept it, because it can do nothing else, is fatal, on the one side to human dignity and on the other to the quality of human character, since, as someone has said: "It makes the top dog a bull and the under dog a cur."

The same general characteristics are as recognizable in militarist politics within the nation as in the international field. It is not by accident that Prussian and Bismarckian conceptions in foreign policy are invariably accompanied by autocratic conceptions in internal affairs. Both are founded upon a belief in force as the ultimate determinant in human conduct; a disbelief in the things of the mind as factors of social control, a disbelief in moral forces that cannot be expressed in "blood and iron." The impatience shown by the militarist the world over at government by discussion, his desire to "shut up the talking shops" and to govern autocratically, are but expressions of the same temper and attitude.

That temper and attitude have, of course, profoundly affected the whole course of social history, and are affecting it to-day. The forms which Governments have taken and the general method of social management are in large part the result of its influence. Most Governments are to-day framed far more as instruments for the exercise of physical force than as instruments of social management.

Now, the militarist attitude would have one justification if it were true that the mind of man is incapable of discerning how his conduct shall be shaped, if man were, like other animals, merely part of the blind forces of nature; if in his acts there could be no element of intelligent volition—then the mechanical hazard of blind force would be as good a test to which to put social policy as any.

And this, indeed, is the fundamental assumption, however little avowed or even recognized, of militarist philosophy. It is betrayed in the common habit of talking of war as one talks of earthquake or pestilence, as "coming upon us"—not as something that we create. The following passage from a much-quoted military writer (General Homer Lea) reveals what is the most significant note of all similar literature:

"National entities, in their birth, activities, and death, are controlled by the same laws that govern all life—plant, animal, or national. Plans to thwart them, to shortcut them, to circumvent, to cozen, to deny, to scorn and violate them, is folly such as man's conceit alone makes possible. Never has this been tried—and man is ever at it—but what the end has been gangrenous and fatal.

"In theory international arbitration denies the inexorability of natural laws, and would substitute for them the veriest Caghostroic formulas, or would, with the vanity of Canute, sit down on the ocean-side of life and command the ebb and flow of its tides to cease.

"The idea of international arbitration as a substitute for natural laws that govern the existence of political entities arises not only from a denial of their fiats and an ignorance of their application, but from a total misconception of war, its causes and its meaning."

General Lea's thesis is emphasised in the introduction to his work, written by another American soldier, General John J. P. Storey:

"A few idealists may have visions that with advancing civilization war and its dread horrors will cease. Civilization has not changed human nature. The nature of man makes war inevitable. Armed strife will not disappear from the earth until human nature changes."

Thus, the militarist does not allow that man has free will in the matter of his conduct at all; he insists that mechanical forces on the one side or the other alone determine which of two given courses shall be taken; the ideas which either, or both, hold, the rôle of intelligent volition, apart from their influence in the manipulation of physical force, play no real part in human society. "Prussianism," Bismarckian "blood and iron," are merely political expressions of this belief in the social field—the belief that force alone can decide things; that it is not man's business to question authority in politics or authority in the form of inevitability in nature. It is not a question of who is right, but of who is stronger. "Fight it out, and right will be on the side of the victor"—on the side, that is, of the heaviest metal or the heaviest muscle, or, perhaps, on that of the one who has the sun at his back, or some other advantage from external nature. The blind material things—not the seeing mind and the soul of man—are the ultimate sanction of human society.

Such a doctrine, of course, is not only profoundly anti-social: it is anti-human—fatal not merely to better international relations, but, in the end, to the degree to which it influences human conduct at all, to all those large freedoms which man has so painfully won. And yet it is an integral part of the militarist outlook. It is entirely what we would expect, that the most warlike people now occupying Europe—those whose presence here has no justification save that of military force, and whose history has been called a "catalogue of battles," because, there is nothing else in it—should be also the most fatalistic of all European populations.

This philosophy makes of man's acts, not something into which there enters the element of moral responsibility and free volition, something apart from and above the mere mechanical force of external nature, but it makes man himself a helpless slave; it implies that his moral efforts and the efforts of his mind and understanding are of no worth—that he is no more the master of his conduct than the tiger of his, or the grass and trees of theirs; and no more responsible.

To this philosophy, the civilist opposes another: that in man there is that which sets him apart from the plants and the animals, which gives him control of and responsibility for his social acts; which makes him the master of his social destiny if he but will it; that by virtue of the forces of his mind he may go forward to the completer conquest, not merely of nature, but of himself, and thereby, and by that alone, redeem human association from the evils that now burden it.

Arms and Industry

A Study of

The Foundations of International Polity

I

THE CASE FOR THE REVISION OF CERTAIN PRINCIPLES OF STATECRAFT

(An address delivered in the Great Hall of the University of Würtzburg, to a meeting of Students convened by the Rektor, Feb. 13, 1913.)*

IT is hardly necessary, I take it, in a great centre of German learning, to labour the point that the correction of any widespread misconception touching large human issues, or the correction of any misinterpretation of facts or false reasoning concerning them, is desirable in itself, and is its own justification, even when the immediate practi-

* The substance of this lecture was also delivered to students in the Universities of Berlin, Leipzig, Göttingen, Heidelberg and Munich as well as at New College, Oxford.

cal import is not apparent. We assume that the real student desires, in his field of learning, to see things as they are, knowing that, if his interpretation of one group of facts is radically wrong, his interpretation of all other related facts whatsoever will be to some extent distorted: he will have to twist them in a lesser or greater degree to make them fit the first distortion. And though to correct a given error may have no direct bearing on practical affairs, that correction will certainly affect the interpretation of other facts which may have a very important practical bearing.

Yet all such corrections, all new interpretations have had to struggle against the view either that their recognition is practically unimportant, or that it may lead to the undermining of some large body of general doctrine, the retention of which is deemed of great practical importance. Probably all that the contemporaries of Galileo could see in his contentions, in the Copernican controversy, was that they tended to discredit an ancient and venerable faith for a perfectly futile thing, the demonstration that the position or the movements of the world on which we live were not what they had been thought to be—"As though our opinion concerning it could alter the thing one way or another," we can imagine the "practical" man of his time declaring. And nearly five hundred years later, when Darwin gave another new interpretation of facts, the real attitude both of the academic world and the practical man was very similar: it was felt that to leave undisturbed the ancient doctrines concerned so deeply with the daily life and conduct of men, and upon which mankind had learned to lean for guidance, was infinitely more important than the discussion of a merely zoölogical or even biological truth, which had no direct bearing upon life and conduct.

Yet we now realize that in these cases, as in numberless similar ones that have come between, both of the popular assumptions I have indicated were wrong. The full recognition of the new truths did not involve the collapse of the general body of the old doctrine—it left all that was of real value therein undisturbed; and it did have very great, incalculable practical value. Just imagine the general opinion of Galileo's times having been triumphant, the new heresy successfully extirpated, and the geocentric hypothesis imposed as a dogma not to be questioned, with all that told against it suppressed. It is certainly not too much to say that such success of the popular and orthodox view would have made impossible the modern world as we now know it, reposing as it does upon a basis of organised knowledge, with huge populations dependent for their very daily food upon the use of such organised knowledge in the exploitation of the universe. So with Darwin's work. It would be a very ignorant person indeed to-day who would dismiss it with the gibe so common a generation since, about men and monkeys and our grandfathers' tails. We know that the hypothesis has profoundly affected our conceptions in an immense area of human knowledge, and by so doing has affected human society and conduct in very many fields.

Now, this attitude, which academic authority and popular opinion have almost invariably assumed towards the correction of error during the last five hundred years in Europe, is precisely the attitude now adopted towards attempts that have been made by a small band of men in Europe of late to correct certain errors in prevailing political and economic ideas. Because the discussion of those ideas has been associated in the past mainly with the effort to secure international peace, the "man of the day," as someone has called him (or the "man of yesterday," as I should prefer to call him), can only think of the discussion as concerned with an effort to avoid fighting; the promulgation of a doctrine based on a readiness to take risks in the matter of our country's safety and interest in order to avoid sacrifices, which, however sad because involving suffering to innocent parties, are made readily enough in the field of industry and commerce. This "man of the day" is apt to feel that a doctrine, the prompting motive of which is the avoidance of suffering, and which, to attain that end, will throw discredit upon instincts of patriotism that are sacred and precious even above human life, cannot make any very deep appeal, especially when we remember that more lives are sacrificed to industry than to war. No one suggests that we should not bridge continents with railroads and seas with ships, because in so doing we sacrifice lives with a certainty as great as though we condemned, by our deliberate act, thousands of men to be crushed to death or drowned or burnt alive.

I think it is quite fair to say this: that to very many Peace advocacy appears as made up in part by a recoil from the sacrifice of lives, which, however, is considerably less than that which he sees going on around him every day in the interests merely of material wealth—a sacrifice which in that case excites no protest; and in part by disparagement of such things as national safety and honour, which he regards as of infinitely greater worth than the industries and commerce which take a heavier toll of life than does war. And consequently, looking at what would be achieved by the change and what is jeopardised by it, he opposes to all ideas which seem even remotely to be concerned with schemes of international peace, either a ferocious hostility which he feels ought to be excited by all doctrines that imply indifference to his country's safety and interests, or a tolerant contempt which he would mete out to all sentimental or academic futility, just as five hundred years ago, he dismissed the "theories" of Galileo with some reference to everybody standing on their heads, and fifty years ago the theories of Darwin by some reference to monkeys and their tails.

May I say that, if the case for Pacifism were what I have just indicated, if really its object were merely the avoidance of suffering, to be obtained at the price of national jeopardy, his attitude would be entirely justified; and I hope you will not think me callous if I say that did Pacifism offer nothing more than the mere avoidance of that physical suffering which war involves, you would not find me here to-night. Because the word "peace" generally connotes this narrow objective, and leaves aside altogether what is really implied in our attempt to correct what we believe to be very deep-seated errors in human relationship, I almost wish that that word could never be used. Just as Galileo knew that the real justification of his attempt to correct prevailing error was not a trivial point as to the exact place or shape of the planet on which we live, but the right understanding of the physical universe, its laws and nature; so do we know that our case is bound up with the destruction of misconceptions which distort and falsify the fundamental principles on which human society is based.

What I have to urge upon your attention, therefore, is not the desirability of "Peace" in the sense of the cessation of conflict, still less of a cosmopolitanism which asks that you shall, in obedience to some abstract ideal of instinctive or intuitive origin, sacrifice national preferences and characteristics, or even prejudices; or of any other cut-and-dried political doctrine or dogma. If "Peace" and "Internationalism" meant what they are generally taken to mean, the whole thing would leave me cold. But I want to urge the consideration of certain facts and forces, the significance of which is for the most part ignored, although they must profoundly affect principles of action between men that cover the whole field of human association, affect to some extent the form and character of all our social structure; which have a very practical bearing upon prevailing conceptions in morals, legislation, jurisprudence, political science generally, economics, law, and the interpretation of history. Their full realization may, indeed, tend to bring into relief certain general principles in the mechanism of society which, if sound, may do as great a service in the improvement of social action as that done in the improvement of thought four or five centuries since by the general adoption—or revival—of the inductive method of reasoning. It is not a question for the moment where the conclusions upon which the study I have in mind may point—(though I want you to believe that no political, religious, national, or sentimental prepossessions of any kind have weighed in my own case, and that I would as readily have drawn, if the facts had pointed thereto, exactly contrary conclusions, and by no means have been frightened therefrom by the rattle of the sabre)—but, if you are concerned at all with the large issues I have indicated, I do not think you can afford to ignore the bearing of the forces in question.

Nor should you conclude from the illustrations that I have just employed, and the emphasis I have laid on the importance of the indirect effects of the principles I want you to investigate, that their direct effect is insignificant. However much we may be divided in other aspects of the problem of war and national defence, we are all accustomed to say, whether we believe it or not, that those problems are both morally and materially the most important of our generation. And yet we find that in this problem we are not facing facts; that we proceed habitually upon assumptions which analysis does not support, that we are ignoring changes which have taken place, and basing our action daily upon conceptions which have become obsolete, upon unrealities, sometimes upon shams.*

*Dr. David Jayne Hill, who was the United States Ambassador to Germany, has emphasized this stagnation in the Science of Statecraft in these terms:

"However radical the transformation of the nature of political power may be, nothing is so difficult as to modify its traditions. . . Many diplomatists and statesmen who count themselves strictly orthodox still consider it impossible to establish any other permanent relations between States than those of mutual fear and distrust; which have, they claim, always existed between nations, and must exist for ever. They hold that history confirms their doctrine; and that States, in whatever form they have existed, are mere temporary and local means for repressing within themselves the aggressive and avaricious instincts of human nature; and that these instincts are destined forever to break forth in some new form of ferocity and destruction, unless they are held firmly in the leash by the hand of power. Statesmen of this school of thought have little faith in any form of self-govern-

You cannot get to the bottom of War and the conceptions out of which it arises without taking stock in some degree of all social and political ideas, without putting them to a new test. And no sound idea can suffer from being put to a new test; all ideas are likely to be improved by it; it is the only means by which fallacies are corrected. If what we are urging with reference to international politics is broadly true, then in much of our general political action, not merely with reference to one group in its relation to another group, but also to a large extent with reference to the relations of men individually to other men, we are misunderstanding some of the fundamental principles which must govern their life in communities in order to insure the best conditions for them: are misunderstanding the mechanism of human society, misreading the means by which we wring our substance from the earth, failing to seize the arrangement most advantageous for the purpose of carrying on our war with nature.

I think that point can be made plain immediately if we get clearly in our minds the nature of

ment, regard the idea of justice as a purely abstract and unrealizable ideal, and consider law as a more or less arbitrary restraint upon the mass, imposed by great masters, against whose authority the natural man is in an attitude of endless secret revolt."

The view of the "classic diplomatists," as Hill calls them, is indeed the antithesis of that development of Locke's theory which would regard the whole system of social organization, not as something "imposed from above by superior power, but something developed from within by the free rational activity of man in response to his imperative social needs."

that main conception, the fundamental assumption concerning the relationship of states, at present universally accepted, which we challenge.

That assumption is not always very clear because its statement almost always takes a negative form. Thus Major Stewart Murray:

> "A nation's only hope of enduring peace, so long as it has anything worth taking from it, depends upon it possessing defensive forces sufficient to give an assailant no reasonable hope of success. . . Peace depends upon the armed force of the nations."*

To say "Peace depends upon the armed force of the nations" is exactly equivalent to saying: "If the nations had no armies how murderously they would go to war with one another! If they had no battleships, naval engagements between them could not be prevented; the armies without soldiers and with no weapons would be annihilating; without horses the cavalry charges would be terrible, without guns the artillery duels appalling." The author means, of course, that Peace depends upon the armed forces not being used, and to prevent our rival's force being used against us we are compelled to oppose an equivalent force so as to cancel it, and to obtain a result which would be obtained with far more certainty if there were no forces that either the one or the other could use. If neither resorted to armed force, the peace would not—could not—be broken.

* "Future Peace of the Anglo Saxon," p. 13. (Watts & Co.)

But the most important point about this passage is that it implies as a thing so deep-seated and evident as not to be worth discussion, a universal belief in the advantage of military aggression.

Why is it certain, in the view of this author, that force will be used "if there is reasonable hope of success"? Because, presumably, it would be advantageous to do so. I am not aware that anyone has yet argued that foreign nations are going to attack us from altruistic motives—for our good.

It is the belief in the advantage of successful attack that creates armed force—armies—and so creates the armies of defence to resist them.

If each is threatened, it is because we all believe that military force can be used to promote an interest, and consequently will, in the case of others, be so used unless we can prevent it. At the bottom of the whole system of orthodox statecraft is the assumption that advantage accrues to successful aggression, and that, as Admiral Mahan tells us: "It is vain to expect nations to act consistently from any motive other than that of interest. . . . And the predatory instinct that he should take who has the power survives."

Now, whether it is true that it is vain to expect nations to act otherwise than from motives of interest I am not for the moment concerned to show. I *am* concerned to show that that is the assumption of orthodox statecraft, with which is associated necessarily the further assumption that spoliation of rivals is to the interest of nations. If spoliation were not presumed to be to their interest, we should not be in danger of it.

If we can keep the positive instead of the negative form of the proposition before us, the thing becomes much clearer: we must defend ourselves because conquest, spoliation, is advantageous.

What does conquest, spoliation, imply? It implies that it is more advantageous to turn our efforts to taking another nation's wealth than to creating our own; that if we can obtain power of coercion over other men we can compel them in some form or other to work for us instead of for themselves, either by paying us tribute or giving conditions in trade which they would not give us unless compelled; that they can be made to surrender a portion of the product of their labour which they would not surrender of their own free will; that the thing really prized by the nations is the power of coercing others; that this tendency to acquire power of coercion is operating all the time with others, and that we must be in a position to cancel it.

This belief in the value of the power of coercion is at the bottom, not only of orthodox statecraft, of the belief in the advantage of conquest, but equally of the belief in the advantages of political privilege, just as it was at the bottom of the belief in slavery and still cruder forms of spoliation.

Now, I take the ground that an examination of the facts, of the results yielded by this general method in the case of nations, as compared with the results yielded by a certain other method, shows this assumption to be false, mistaken: not, will you note, that it is "*immoral*,"—that is another story—but false, judged in the light of those motives of interest which we are told by the defenders of the system are its foundation.

I want, as an introduction to the study of this subject, to give you a hint of certain mechanical forces that are necessarily set in motion, as soon as men begin to co-operate, by so apparently simple a device as the division of labour; of the process by which these forces so act as progressively to nullify the efficacy of the physical coercion of one party to the division of labour, by another, rendering our current estimate of the worth, whether moral or material, of coercion false, because it ignores the weight of these forces.

I want to show first that this mode of social action,—according to which it is to our interest to act indirectly against the forces of Nature, that is to say, first by using our energy to secure power over someone else, and then using that power to compel him to apply *his* energy to Nature—is uneconomic in the larger sense of the term; it represents a waste of human effort.

The exercise of coercion over other men necessarily presumes resistance (if there is no resistance coercion is not necessary). The energy expended is met by the resistance of the "coercee," and to the extent to which such resistance is effective you get merely a cancellation of force or energy, which is, of course, quite unproductive. I will try by illustration to make clear what may be obscure in abstract definition.

Here are two men: one is digging; the other is standing over him with a whip or a weapon. We are apt to think of one as bond, and the other as free; but both are bond. If the man with the whip or weapon is thirsty, and wants to go to the river to drink, he cannot: his slave would run away. He is sleepy and wants to sleep, equally he cannot. He would like to hunt; equally he cannot. He is bound, tied to the slave much as the slave is tied to him. His work of control, compulsion, watching, whatever you care to call it, is not directly productive at all; it is only indirectly productive, necessitated by the resistance of the slave. If we can imagine the slave driver or owner, wearied with this arrangement, saying to the slave—"I am going hunting, and if you will stay here and do this task during the day, I will give you half of the proceeds of my hunt," and the slave agreeing to this, you double the productivity of the two men; you have two producing instead of one. Indeed, you have more, because if the offer is such as really to involve a voluntary agreement on the part of the slave—a desire to do the work in order to get the reward—all the energy which the slave originally devoted to looking for a chance of escape is now liberated for his task. This is the economic case against slavery, as at bottom it is the economic case against robbery, conquest, and every other form of human coercion, which means to some degree always the cancelling of energy by resistance, instead of its fruitful use against Nature, which is the final source of all wealth however obtained.

I can illustrate a further development of this thesis in another way. Here are two tribes of one hundred men each living on opposite sides of a river, both engaged in growing corn or some other simple form of agriculture. It occurs one day to one of the tribes that it would be much simpler to go and take the corn of the other tribe than to labour at growing corn themselves. So some fifty of the best-trained men sally forth to despoil their neighbours. The second tribe resist: some of the fifty are killed, a portion of the corn is captured. The first tribe then argue that they did not employ force enough, and they begin to increase the number of their fighting men and, by definite training, their efficiency. The second tribe, determined not again to be the victims of spoliation, do the same, and you start a competition of armaments, with this result, that at the next foray, you find seventy-five men of the first tribe ranged in battle against seventy-five men of the second. We will assume that the first tribe is successful, beats the seventy-five of the defenders—who, like themselves, have been devoting their energies to warlike training, and not to the production of grain—and as the result of their victory they capture grain produced by twenty-five men. Thus, the result of labour (in warlike preparations, the production of weapons, training, etc.), of seventy-five men yields the amount of wealth represented by the labour of twenty-five men. Would not the result have been exactly three times as great if their force had been turned directly against Nature instead of using it against men?

But that by no means covers, even in fundamental principle, the whole of the case. It will have occurred to you, of course, that the embryo of society is to be found in the division of labour. If we were not compelled to divide our labour, if in order to get what we want it were not necessary for one to do one thing and one another, not only would there be no trade and commerce—there would be no courts of law, no society at all. If each could really suffice for himself, without the co-operation of others, we should be just in the condition of the herbivorous animals, feeding upon the plants, indifferent as to whether all other individuals of their own species disappear or not—truly independent, truly self-sufficing, and therefore with no obligations to others, and others having no obligations to us. But from the moment that we wear clothes, or eat bread, or have our teeth filled, or our appendix removed, we cease to be independent, we cease to be indifferent to the disappearance of others of our species: really we cannot remove our own appendix. And if you make even a cursory list of the number of people that are necessary to supply your clamant daily needs, you will find, of course, that they number not half a dozen, or a dozen, or even hundreds, but if you make the calculation correctly, hundreds of thousands. And if you have ever dreamed dreams of an ideal world in which you would live as part of some simple village community, independent of the rest of the world, I wonder whether you have fully considered all that is meant by the surrendering of such things as literature, music, books, being able to hear from your friends and writing to them, having an anæsthetic when your leg is to be removed as the result of an accident, saving your women from excessive labour—for in all ideal village communities the women are old at twenty-five, as the result of unceasing physical fatigue—of seeing something of the world, or keeping your mother's portrait when she is dead? For if you are not prepared to give up these things, if you desire even the smallest proportion of them, you must resign yourself to the existence of a complex community, and to communication with foreign countries, invention, laboratories, scientific investigation. And if you calculate all that this means, you will find that you are depending, not upon this little community, but upon hundreds of thousands, millions of men, whom you have never seen and never can see, many living on the other side of the world, dependent upon them, it may be, for your very existence, as I shall shortly show.

But the important thing in this is that by division of labour you have created a condition of dependence upon others, and that dependence upon others necessarily implies a limitation of the force which you can use against these others. Even in slavery, if the master is dependent upon the labour of the slaves, the force he can use against them is limited—he cannot kill them. As the division of labour increases in complexity, a progressive stultification of force takes place, as I have detailed elsewhere.

The fact that complete interdependence means the complete stultification of force is illustrated by the position of two men in a boat of whom I read once in a book of adventure. The boat was leaky, the sea heavy, and the shore a long way off. It took all the efforts of the one man to row, and of the other to bale. If either had ceased both would have drowned. At one point the rower threatened the baler that if he did not bale with more energy he would throw him overboard; to which the baler made the obvious reply that, if he did, he (the rower) would certainly drown also. And as the rower was really dependent upon the baler, and the baler upon the rower, neither could use force against the other. The threat of death itself became ineffective in such circumstances.

To the degree then to which interdependence is complete, force becomes ineffective.

But I want to indicate certain other factors that operate. Imagine two villages separated for most months of the year by an impenetrable swamp. In this condition each village is compelled to produce nearly all that it needs itself—the condition of most villages in Europe a generation or two ago. But imagine that the swamp has been cut by a canal, and that the situation of one of these villages is particularly suitable for the production of foodstuffs, and the other for the production of metals and fuel. What will inevitably happen is that, as the result of this improvement in communication and cheapening of transport, one village will be mainly engaged upon producing foodstuffs, and the other upon producing coal and iron. In a greater or lesser degree they will make an exchange of their products. Now, in the first condition, where there was no exchange, and where each village produced all that it needed, one can imagine the men of the first village attacking the second, raiding it, carrying off its goods, and not themselves suffering by the annihilation even of the second village. (It was the condition of border villages a century or two ago.) But after the construction of the canal, when the improvement of communication has led them to divide their labour, it would serve little purpose for the miners to wage war against the food-producers; and if in doing so they wiped them out in the old-fashioned way, they would be threatened by starvation. And the condition of interdependence would be none the less even if it were indirect—that is to say, if one village, mainly agricultural, annoyed at paying too much for its implements, raided a second village where they were made, and ruined the purchasing power of this village so that it could no longer buy the coal of a third village which happened to be the main market of the agriculturists of the first village. Although you may find your market in consumer A, you will ruin it, perhaps, by attacking B, upon whom A is dependent.

Now, you know, of course, that that is the condition of the modern world. The intercommunication exemplified by the canal, which renders possible the extension of the division of labour as between otherwise separated communities, and without which such division of labour is not possible, is the characteristic factor of our time. I think it is certainly true to say that one hundred years ago communication was less effective in Europe than it had been two thousand years previously. But this last one hundred years has drawn capitals at opposite sides of the world more closely together, and placed them in more intimate communication than neighbouring country towns in the same State were in before the day of steam and telegraphy. And yet we assume that the relationships between these groups, transformed as they must be by this marvellous new element of interdependence, are exactly what they were before it existed. I am not exaggerating. It is positively laid down by our greatest authorities on the relations of nations, that the factor of power, of force, is what it was in the days of Cæsar, of Machiavelli, of Clauserwitz; that of fundamental change there is none. Yet the factor of communication represents progressive and dynamic forces which must fundamentally transform the relationships between the communities affected by them. That canal, obviously representing a revolution in the relationship of those two villages, is yet declared by the wise men of those two villages in no way to affect that relationship!

It is, of course, not the mere fact of contact which has rendered them interdependent but the division of labour which that improvement of communication has brought about—the new fact that the prosperity of either of these communities is conditional upon the due performance of its functions by the other.

Not only does existing political and economic literature still employ the terminology of international conditions which have in fact disappeared, but the underlying ideas of such literature ignore characteristic developments of our time. If one compares an average modern treatise on a problem of international politics—whether it takes the form of a leading article in a newspaper or the more pretentious treatment of a Quarterly Review, or the books of any recognized authority on the subject—with a corresponding treatise of the eighteenth century it will be found that the terminology and ideas are fundamentally identical, the evident assumption on the part of the twentieth-century writer being that the essential facts of the problem have not changed. Yet the facts have so changed as to render what were axioms in the eighteenth century absurdities in the twentieth.

The whole case of the relation of military power to social and economic advantage, the extent to which the general well-being of one group can be advanced by military domination over another, or to which the interlacing of interests checks the useful or effective imposition of such domination, demands restatement in the terms of the developments of the last thirty or forty years.

Take, for instance, the general assumptions—

1. That conquered territory adds to the wealth of the conquering nation; that it can be "owned" in the way that a person or a corporation would own an estate;
2. That military power is a means of imposing upon other countries economic conditions favourable to the nation exercising it;
3. That nations are economic units—"competing business firms," as one great military authority recently called them;

and test their reality by the facts—

1. That wealth in conquered territory remains in the hands of the inhabitants; special

taxation or tribute being a Roman or feudal contrivance, more and more difficult of application to, and unprofitable in, modern administrative methods by reason of that intangibility of wealth, which mutual dependence of peoples, due to the division of labour cutting across frontiers, has brought about.

2. That the economic conditions in lesser States (*e. g.*, Sweden, Holland, Belgium, Switzerland) are just as good as in the States exercising great military power (*e. g.*, Russia, Germany, Austria). That the foreign trade of most great States is mainly with countries over which they exercise no political control. Great Britain does twice as much trade with foreign countries as with her Colonies (which she does not control). The enormous expansion of German trade, mainly in countries like Russia, the United States, South America, owes nothing to her military power.

3. That great industrial nations are not economic units; international trade is not exchanged between corporations known as "Britain," "Germany," etc., but is a process of complex operations divided infinitely between individuals; a Birmingham ironmaster sells his engines to

> a Brazilian coffee-planter, who is able to buy them because he sells his coffee to a merchant in Havre, who sells it to a Westphalian town manufacturing rails for Siberia, which buys them because peasants are growing wheat as the result of the demand in Lancashire, which is manufacturing cotton for Indian coolies growing tea for sheep-farmers in Australia, who are able to buy it because they sell wool to a Bradford merchant, who manufactures it because he is able to sell cloth to a petroleum-refiner in Baku, who is able to buy good clothing because he is selling petrol to the users of automobiles in Paris. How can such an operation, which is typical of most international trade, be described as the competition of rival units—such as Great Britain, Germany, France, Brazil, or Russia?

And these very simple facts our most pretentious statecraft ignores. Until they are better understood there can be no permanent solution of what are the most insistent and pressing problems of our time, no advance towards a better general condition.

Now, I am talking, I hope, to good Germans—that is to say, to men who if they had to choose between the interests of their fellow-countrymen and the interests of strangers would choose the interests of their countrymen. In the same way I hope I am a good Englishman, in the sense that if I had to make a similar choice I would decide unhesitatingly in the favour of those who touch me nearly in my daily life, to whom I have a definite and visible responsibility, in preference to those who, on my part, I do not know and cannot know. If I believed that there was a conflict of interests between Great Britain and Germany, I should be for Great Britian and against Germany. And if the doctrines most in favour with the political philosophers, the statesmen, the newspaper writers, of our respective countries, are true, that conflict is inevitable. So long as Britons believe that their wealth and power can be lost and transferred to another nation as the result of a single naval defeat, so long as Germans believe that they will always be excluded from their fair share of the world's wealth unless they are able to back their claims by force, why, inevitably, there will be a competition for the possession of force. Britons will always reply to any increase in the German navy by a greater increase, and Germans will never be content that a rival nation shall have an overpowering preponderance of force throughout the world. Discussion, even, will hardly be possible; the whole relationship will be coloured by the feeling that our interests are not indeed common, but rival. The outcome is the armament rivalry now in progress. Its risks as well as its limits are obvious. The risks are ill-feeling, suspicion, and temper, and the fact that, in the absence of any necessary cause of dispute, the armaments themselves become one. When an incident like the Dogger Bank affair takes place, war is upon us without either party having planned it or knowing what it is really about. And the practical limits of the policy are equally evident. If our expenditure goes on increasing during the next ten years at the ratio of the last ten years, war itself will become less burdensome than armed peace.

You will, of course, note this, that if those of the newer school are wrong, if nations are necessarily rivals, and must decide their relationship by one dominating the other, then it does not matter whether you give attention to these facts or not. But if we are right—and the curious thing is that whenever our case is studied we are told that we are right—why, then it matters all the world, because then these conflicts are not inevitable at all, not due to any necessary divergence of interests, but chiefly due to the fact that we do not happen to have studied our interests. For note also this,—that wrong opinion about a matter of this kind gives the same resulting action as though the opinion were well founded. If we *falsely* conclude that nations are rivals, we shall fight just as though we really were rivals. But war then becomes simply a question of whether we shall see the facts or fail to see them. And I would also call your attention to this,—that, though you may not draw the conclusions which I draw, the facts upon which I base them concern any policy, any principle of international action, which you may favour, concern indeed all social organization national as much as international.

An English writer, somewhat of the Clauserwitz school, lays down this rule:

> A prudent statesman, before letting himself be drawn into a quarrel with another State, will take pains to reach a true estimate of the importance of the point in dispute, both to his own State and to the antagonist; for in proportion as a community finds its being and its well-being bound up with a particular purpose, the more intense and persistent will be its exertions for the assertion of that purpose. If then, I commit my people to a war for something that turns out to be a mere whim, they will sooner or later grow tired of the struggle; and if the conditions on which I propose to insist involve the ruin of the State opposed to me, the people of that State will only grow more determined and more desperate as the struggle proceeds. This disparity of motive for exertion may go far to compensate for almost any degree of inequality between the real strength of the two opponents.

The beginning of war, then, is the purpose in view. From a purpose which is plain you may get a well-conducted war; from a purpose about which you are not clear you never can. Unless you know what you want, you cannot possibly tell whether war is the appropriate way of getting it; therefore, in that case, the decision to go to war is foolish. Moreover, unless you know what you want you can hardly manage your war properly—that is, so as to get what you want. The starting-point of a good war is, therefore, a purpose necessary to your State and clearly understood by your statesmen. Thus, the foundation of success in war is sound policy, without which the greatest generals and the finest armies come to ruin.*

Even, therefore, if you believe that nations are necessarily rivals, and must inevitably fight out their differences by arms, yet nevertheless your policy must take cognisance of the facts to which I appeal.

Now, all those points, which are a necessary part of what I believe is bound to be a definite science, are as much the concern of the nationalist statesman as of the internationalist statesman; as much the concern of those who believe that the employment of military force can be an instrument of national advantage as of those who believe that such means are ineffective, and should be replaced by the international organization of society.

I would indicate a few points on which attention might be centred:

1. How far have modern wealth and trade become intangible as regards military conquest, owing to the development of credit, and the interdependence of economic centres which this involves?

* *War and Policy*, by Prof. Spenser Wilkinson, pp. 394, 395. (Constable, London).

2. To what extent does the greater complexity of the modern industrial organism harass or paralyze the employment of existing military machinery (*e.g.*, could States like Germany feed industrial populations for any considerable period after a general mobilization, the interruption of communications, and the disturbance of the credit system)?
3. To what extent do these factors involve the futility of the employment of military force to commercial ends, and how does the prosperity of the lesser States bear on the general question of the relation of military power and prestige to economic advantage?
4. How far has the development of a cheap press and other means of propaganda and agitation given such strength to local autonomy as to render the imposition of military force in fields other than the economic one impossible (*e.g.*, what lessons are to be drawn from the grant of a constitution to Alsace-Lorraine, the recent breakdown of the French colonial fiscal system, etc.)?

Whatever final conclusion we may draw, the facts are worth more study than, for the most part, they get. To deprecate such study is to argue that, in one of the most difficult problems of our civilization, ignorance and prejudice are better guides than knowledge and wisdom.

Of course, you may take the ground—we are all apt to take this ground, especially, I believe, we English—that if only other nations would act as you act, there would be an end to the problem; that you—or we, for I am merely voicing a point of view that I have heard expressed in exactly identical terms in England, France, America, Austria, Italy, Mexico, Monaco, as well as in Germany—do not desire to commit aggression upon any one, that other nations could all disarm to-morrow with safety so far as you are concerned; that whatever may be the misconceptions which give rise to misunderstandings of interest and conflicts and collisions between nations, you do not share them, and that if only the world had the political wisdom vouchsafed to the British, or the French, or the Germans, or the Austrians, or the Americans, or the Mexicans, or Monagasque, as the case may be, international problems would disappear; that, when we talk of the inevitable struggle for life among nations, we mean that it is only the other nations that are struggling; when our Homer Leas or Bernhardis talk of the universal law of conflict, of human passion and pugnacity, they mean that the nation of the writer is exempted by Providence from universal law and universal passion. You may say that when these masters of statecraft lay down with such dogmatism that each State is necessarily a "predatory entity, restrained only by the resistance that it may encounter," they refer only to *other* States.

If you say this "basic assumption" of state craft, as De Gartden calls it, is not that we should act in such a way, but that is the way we must expect others to act towards us, then we do nevertheless believe that such is the prevailing doctrine, but that we happen to be free from an error which enslaves the rest of the world. It is a little difficult to discuss politics on the basis that Providence has so created us as to be free from error common to all foreigners; but even if we take that view, it is evident that our burden is the direct result of prevailing error, since we are compelled to do our part in the maintenance of a general system in which we do not believe, because others are mistaken as to what it can accomplish—and it is also evident that we have a direct interest in the destruction of such error by the exposure of the misconceptions which have provoked it. And if you take the ground that it is no good our interesting ourselves in the matter, since it is the foreigners who are the fools, as Dr. Johnson would have said, then you take the ground that German intellectual influence—or British I should say if I were talking to a British audience—is of no weight in the world, that the political thought of one group does not affect that of another, that British Parliamentary government has not influenced the general form of representative government throughout the world, that the French Revolution and the ideas which preceded it and provoked it had nothing to do with that movement of the generation that followed it—the revolt of Spanish America, the movement which swept through the Italian States, as well as the German states and put Europe and the Western Hemisphere in the melting-pot. We are to assume that Karl Marx had nothing to do with the Socialistic ferment that permeated, in the generation that followed *him*, most of Western Europe; or, if you go into other fields, that Luther played no part in religious thought outside the town of Wurtemberg, Calvin outside that of Geneva, or that Darwin only transformed "English" biology, whatever that might be.

Did you ever know a single idea that mattered in the affairs of men—whether in the field of industry, or medicine, or philosophy, or politics, or sociology, or, for that matter, in dress or diet or entertainment—that could for long remain the exclusive possession of a single nation in the Western World? Yet we take the ground that a conception fundamentally affecting some of the greatest problems of life can animate the minds of forty million British or sixty million Germans more or less, and have no effect upon the minds and conduct of the rest of the world.

Such a condition—that the knowledge and ideas of one group do not affect the conduct and character of others, that advance is not the common work of mankind but is a matter of separate and independent acts—has never been true of any period of written history, and is certainly not more likely to be true of ours than of previous periods. The moral and intellectual interdependence of mankind long antedates its material or economic interdependence; it has been an outstanding factor in the development of all past civilizations, and is certainly not likely to play a smaller rôle in ours. Indeed, it is just the simple truth to say that we all owe our civilization to foreigners, that if each of us could have excluded "foreign" ideas from our political groups our civilization would still be represented by the stone axe and the cave dwelling —a simple matter of fact which certain reactionary tendencies in political philosophy and a very pernicious terminology have done a good deal to obscure.

As an Englishman, for instance, I have to make a definite effort properly to realize that our commerce and political institutions, the sanctity of the English home, and all the other things upon which we pride ourselves, are the result of anything but the unaided efforts of a long line of Englishmen. One has to stop and uproot impressions that are almost instinctive, to remember that but for the trick of growing grains and plants for food, which our distant and common forefathers learnt of Asia, the chief British industry might still be the manufacture of flint hatchets; that we sail the ships of our world-wide commerce by the virtue of knowledge which we owe to the astronomical researches of Egyptians and Chaldeans, who inspired the astronomers of Greece, who inspired those of the Renaissance in Italy, Spain, and Germany, keeping alive and developing not merely the art of measuring space and time but also that conception of order in external nature without which the growth of organized knowledge, which we call science enabling men to carry on their exploitation of the world, would have been impossible; that our very alphabet comes from Rome, who owed it to others; that the mathematical foundation of our modern mechanical science—without which neither Newton, nor Watts, nor Stevenson, nor Faraday could have been—is the work of Arabs,* strengthened by Greeks, protected and enlarged by Italians; that our conceptions of political organization which have so largely shaped our political science come mainly from the Scandinavian colonists of a French province; that English intellect has been nurtured mainly by Greek philosophy; that English law is principally Roman, and English religion entirely Asiatic in its origins; that for the thing which we deem to be the most important concerning us, our spiritual and religious aspirations, we go to a Jewish book interpreted by a Church Roman in origin, reformed mainly by the efforts of Swiss and German theologians; that the Royal Family, which is the symbol of intensely

*So widespread was Arab influence at one period in Europe that the English King Offa had his coinage stamped with Arabic inscriptions, as Arabic measures of money were those chiefly used by merchants throughout Europe at that time.

English nationalism, has for nearly two hundred years spoken German more readily than English.

But then, of course, we are a particularly insular people, afraid to construct the Channel Tunnel for fear that our insularity should be diminished and that we should suffer from foreign contamination.

Do you not see that this notion that our intellectual activity can have no influence upon foreigners is an intellectual abdication simply inexplicable coming from the mouths of patriots, from those who profess to glory in the big rôle that their country plays in the affairs of the world? If we are completely right, and the foreigners completely wrong; if we have such natural wisdom in the matter that our vision, clear and pellucid, pierces these old illusions that have so long deceived and entrapped humanity—then it is high time we imparted some of this wisdom to the benighted foreigner, and taught him something of the secret by which we have grasped the truth while he is still sunk in ignorance. We have no right, as we have certainly no interest, to keep it to ourselves.

For these burdens of ours, if this view is right, are the result of their ignorance.

As a matter of simple fact, of course, in the domain of ideas that matter, there are no political frontiers. The ideas which make European civilization are common to the whole, and all those factors of improved communication which have intensified our material interdependence have to a still greater degree intensified our moral and intellectual interdependence.

To certain phases of this problem eminent Germans are happily already beginning to turn their attention. Men like Bernard Harms of Kiel have approached the subject from a point of view similar to mine; while in the sciences from which this new science must so largely draw—economics, law, and social organization—Germany in some respects leads the world. One has only to mention the names of Lujo Brentano, Karl von Bar, Wilhelm Ostwald, Hans Wehberg, Piloty, Schücking, to realize that Germany has in these and other intellectual leaders the wherewithal to make a preponderant contribution to this Political Reformation of Europe, especially, if I may be allowed to say so, on the side of systematization and organization, in which the genius of modern Germany excels.

I have uttered the phrase "Political Reformation." Former generations of Europeans fought far more bitterly over religious differences than we are likely to fight again over political differences. These wars were stopped not by what I may term "mechanical means," by conventions, treaties, the imposition of the preponderant power of any one group, but simply by the rationalization of general opinion, which in its turn was the result of the intellectual ferment created by isolated thinkers and writers of Germany, Italy, Switzerland, France, and Scotland. If these isolated thinkers and writers had not fought for their opinions, that development of the European mind which put a stop to the religious wars would not have taken place, and we should be waging wars of religion yet. The factors which operated to bring to an end the conflicts of the religious groups are the factors which will operate most usefully to bring to an end the conflicts of the political groups. We know the part that German thought and the efforts of a few Germans played in the earlier Reformation. May we not hope that German thought, and the efforts of a few individual Germans, may play a corresponding part in that latter Reformation which I believe is the work of our generation?

II

MORAL AND MATERIAL FACTORS IN INTERNATIONAL POLITICS

(Addresses delivered before the British Association, Dundee, September 5, 1912, and the South Place Institute, (Conway Memorial Lecture), March 18, 1913.)

A DISTINGUISHED American Ambassador, who is at the same time a political writer of great force and originality,* tells us:

"The assumption which lies at the foundation of classic diplomacy is that every State is seeking to appropriate for itself everything in the world that possesses value, and is restrained from actually doing so only by the resistance it may encounter."

In confirmation of that view he quotes, among others, that great pedagogue of diplomacy, the Comte de Gartden, who has outlined the fundamental principles of statecraft for us thus:

"Every State in its external relations has, and can have, no other maxims than these: Whoever, by the

* Dr. David Jayne Hill, who was American Ambassador to Germany.

superiority of his forces and by his geographic position, can do us harm is our natural enemy. Whoever cannot do us harm, but can, by the extent of his forces and by the position he occupies, do injury to our enemy, is our natural friend."

"These propositions," says Ancellon, "are pivots upon which all international intercourse turns." "Fear and distrust"—"indestructible passions," as De Gartden calls them—"prolong the state of open or latent war in which the Powers of Europe live." "The measure of national strength is the only measure of national safety."

Such are the principles on which the system of war statecraft reposes—for they have, as De Gartden shows, the support of all the great classic authorities; they are the commonplaces of the discussion of *la haute politique*, and you know, of course, the superior contempt with which any protest against them on moral grounds has always been met: those who made it were treated as amiable sentimentalists living apart and detached from that world of hard fact where men of ordinary passions lived and moved.

It is rather astonishing, therefore, that when some of us, analyzing the grounds of this cannibalistic political philosophy, declared it to be mistaken and erroneous from the point of view of those motives of interest on which its defenders declare it to be based, we should be told that our view is too sordid for serious discussion!

Thus Admiral Mahan says that all my work is vitiated because I assume self-interest on the part of nations in their politics. He says:

> "To regard the world as governed by self-interest is to live in a non-existent world, an ideal world, a world possessed by an idea much less worthy than those which mankind, to do it bare justice, persistently entertains." *

I am more concerned for the moment, however, with the criticism of those who have never supported the principles which underlay the old diplomacy and statecraft.

Dr. Evans Darby, a veteran of the Peace Movement, to whom I tender my sincerest homage, discussing at a recent Peace Conference a *Quarterly Review* article on "The New Pacifism," protested in these terms: "The common man does not at any time confound morality with material advantage. He knows well—no one better—that they are not always identical, but very often conflicting."

A Professor of a great English University says that war will go on because men are animated by ideas for which they are prepared to die; and so long as they are thus prepared to give their lives for an ideal, possibly quite divorced from any

* This is in criticism of some of my own work. Yet Admiral Mahan, a year or two previously, had said: "It is vain to expect nations to act from any other motives than those of interest." ("The Interest of America in International Conditions," London. Sampson Low.)

material interest whatsoever, the military contest of States will continue. Another very hostile critic says it is absurd to suppose that nations fight about "money," and that it would be a very sad and sordid fact if they did.

And an English Liberal, writing only last week in a morning newspaper, says:

> "I believe that those Pacifists who are relying upon economic arguments, and who are putting into the background the much greater moral and ethical considerations, are doing their case a great disservice."

Now, I suggest that both these ideas—the implication that it is sordid for a community to be guided by self-interest, and that general well-being is distinct from, and even at times in conflict with, morality—are due to confusion of thought, and to the defects and limitations of the terms employed.

"Economics," of course, connotes, not the interests of some persons or a class in the community, but the interests of the whole of the community, and connotes also, not merely money and the coupons of bonds, but the methods by which men earn their bread, and the conditions in which they live. This is not a view special to myself, or to any particular school of economics. Professor Marshall, for instance, in a textbook now nearly fifteen years old, says:

> "Economics is on the one side a study of wealth, and

on the other and more important side a part of the study of man. For man's character has been moulded by his everyday work, and by the material resources which he thereby procures, more than by any other influence, unless it be that of his religious ideals; and the great forming agencies of the world's history have been the religious and the economic. . . . And very often the influence exerted on a person's character by the amount of his income is hardly less, if it is less, than that exerted by the way in which it is earned. It makes little difference to the fulness of life of a family whether its yearly income is £1000 or £5000. But it makes a very great difference whether the income is £30 or £150; for with £150 the family has, with £30 it has not, the material conditions of a complete life. It is true that in religion, in the family affections, and in friendship, even the poor may find scope for many of those faculties which are the source of the highest happiness; but the conditions which surround extreme poverty, especially in densely-crowded places, tend to deaden the higher faculties. Those who have been called the residuum of our large towns have little opportunity for friendship; they know nothing of the decencies and the quiet, and very little of the unity, of family life; and religion often fails to reach them. . . . The study of the causes of poverty is the study of the causes of the degradation of a large part of mankind."*

For, of course, the economic interests of a people mean, not merely food and clothing and habitable

*"The Economics of Industry," pp. 2–3, fourth edition, Macmillan & Co.

houses, the means of decency and cleanliness and good health, but books, education, and some leisure, freedom from care and the cramping terror of destitution, from the effects of the deadly miasma of the slum. The material thing is but the expression of still profounder realities which cannot be separated therefrom, because with leisure and a wider outlook come a finer affection—the laughter of children, the grace of women, some assurance that maternity shall be a joy instead of a burden—the keener feeling for life. Bread is not merely the pulverised seed of a plant, it is the bloom on a child's cheek, it is life; for it is human food—that is to say, a part of what human life represents. And to save for mothers their children, and for men their wives; to prolong human life, to enlarge and dignify it, are aims not to be dismissed as an "appeal to the pocket." And yet they are so dismissed.

So much for the first point—the sordidness of the economic consideration. What of the second—Dr. Evans Darby's—that it is not sufficient to establish the general interest, because morality may be in conflict therewith?

How do you formulate morality? Surely as the observance of that code which best makes for the general interest. If you take the ground that it is not this, but a divine injunction which society must obey even though it destroy society, something dissociated from human ends altogether, I would ask a question or two. How do you account for pagan morality? Is it the divine intention to improve or worsen society? I think we can only answer that the pagan code of morals, so far as it was a sound one, was the recognition, often subconscious, of what made for the general well-being and that a divinity which should desire to make society worse is inconceivable.

No. As a matter of simple fact, we apply this test to all our codes—it is the final appeal: Is it for the well-being, the good, of mankind? If it is, it is moral. If it is not, it is immoral.

You may say: You must define "good" and "well-being." I have defined them. There are certain ultimate realities which spring to one's mind immediately—affection, love, family life, motherhood, fatherhood, the happiness of children; rest after fatigue; achievement after effort—you can prolong the list indefinitely. And these things are bound up with and depend upon more material things—health, which means food and clothing and cleanliness; leisure and serenity, which mean an ordered life, efficiency, the capacity to live in society and to do one's work in the world—and you come back to economics, to sociology, to the science of human society. They are all interdependent parts of one great whole, and you cannot separate them.

So I come back to my definition, that morality is the foundation of the general interest. The connotation of self-sacrifice implied often, too often, I think, in morality and idealism, arises from the fact that, in the general interest, the individual may be called upon to make an apparent sacrifice of his personal material interest. But you cannot, as I have already shown, have such a thing as the sacrifice of the general interest for the sake of the general interest. You come to an absurdity; so that, if it be true that morality is a statement of the general interest, the interest of the community, it follows that interest and morality, when we are talking of communities, must coincide. This, I submit, is Euclidian in its simplicity.

But, you may say, the whole question is the interest of one community as against another; that just as an individual in the nation may have to refrain from a material advantage to himself because it would be at the cost of the general interest, so an individual nation, one of the community of nations, might profit by its force to advantage itself at the cost of others, and would thus be acting immorally, though to its interest.

Now, it is an integral part of the economic case against war that the nation is not the community in the economic sense if there exist international economic relations at all; that it is integrally a part of the whole community of organised society; that to smite the interest of the whole is to smite itself; that, economically, we are part of the general community to the extent of the nation's economic relation with other nations; and if there be no economic relation, actual or prospective, there can be no economic interest, moral or immoral, involved. The shrewdest of those who defend war do so, not merely on the ground that it is to the interest of the victorious nation, but on the ground, also, that it is to the interest of all nations, to mankind in general, by giving the management of the world to the best and ablest elements, and so forth. And, of course, these defenders of war feel they have a moral justification for their faith, just as the Pacifists feel that they have for theirs because they have before them the ultimate well-being of humanity. Thus I have taken the ground that, if we are to know which is right, which is moral, we shall have to determine which really promotes the interest of mankind. My critics reply it is not a question of which promotes the interests, but of which is right. And I say, how are you to test which is right if you disregard the interests of mankind? "Right" then becomes a question of revelation or intuition.

We are told by the older Pacifists that "interest" is not the test; that, though war did "pay," it could still be immoral.

Well, let us see where that leads us. We will assume that the defenders of war who say that it is to the general interest, that it "pays," have judged correctly. Then, according to the older Pacifists, mankind would be materially the better for war, morally worse—a quite possible conclusion, according to Dr. Darby, since the interest and morality of mankind are so often in conflict. That means that every time we fail to go to war we have lost an opportunity of attenuating poverty, of diminishing the mass of hunger, pain, and sickness, among us. The more moral you are as a community in this respect, the worse will your slums become, the more will your teeming population die of consumption, the more will your women be driven by poverty to white slavery, in greater holocausts will your children die. Peace, in terms of human suffering, will be infinitely more cruel than war itself. In short, since morality means, apparently, the opposite of self-interest—that is to say, the sacrifice of self—the community has only to become entirely moral to perish utterly.

Fortunately, there is no such monstrous dilemma, and this criticism of Admiral Mahan, that a community has higher interests than self-interest, and of Dr. Darby, that action which serves self-interest will not serve morality, arises from the old and infinitely mischievous notion that self-interest and morality are at variance, that high ideals must necessarily be in conflict with material advantage, that the higher welfare of the race is in some wonderful way founded upon a sacrifice of its material welfare.

I do not believe that. I believe that morality is not some abstraction to which the conduct of men, to their hurt, must conform, some cruel Kali goddess demanding its human sacrifice, the sacrifice of the great mass of mankind, the lives of children, the tears of women, the health and minds of men, but is, on the contrary, the codification of the general interest; that conduct on the part of the whole which will best serve the interests of the whole, best make for the well-being of society —that is to say, the self-interest of society.

Surely it is the mark of moral progress that the identity between interest and morality becomes clearer, that as man advances in the understanding of human relationship his intelligence bridges this gulf which is supposed to separate self-interest from the ideal motive.

In some story of Indian life occurs an incident which has always stuck in my memory. An Indian saint, living on his handful of rice and fish, has drawn around him on the sand a circle which no one of lower caste may pass if defilement is to be escaped. An English officer crossing the compound allows his shadow to fall within the circle. The Indian saint, faithful to his creed, walks to the river-bank, throws into it the handful of rice and the fish which are his day's food, and goes unfed until the next day, in order that he shall not touch a morsel of what has been defiled by the shadow of the unclean.

One respects this. It is a real sacrifice for a principle—an unquestioned sacrifice simply made. At first thought one would say that a system of morals which had brought out this capacity for sacrifice during untold generations among unnumbered millions of men must be a marvellous vehicle of human improvement. And yet the outcome of it is the Indian civilization we found a century or so ago, and, indeed, find to-day.

In another story of Indian life—Mrs. Steele's *Hosts of the Lord*—I find expressed the very thought here suggested:

> "The rocks themselves had been worn through by the feet of millions who had toiled that painful mountain way to reach the cradle of the gods. And following as far as she could follow in the near hills and the climbing track, worn by the weariness of that eternal search after righteousness, she asked herself what it was that kept mankind so long upon the road. Generation after generation of Eastern pilgrims had worn that path out of the sheer rock, had agonized after good—and had remained evil. A little shudder of memory ran through her at the thought—how evil! And now the West, with its white tents, its white face, its hard way, and its unbelieving mind, had come to show a newer and a better way."

It will have struck you, of course, that the development of religion reveals this curious fact: the early forms are all profoundly permeated by the spirit of self-sacrifice, and by forms of self-sacrifice divorced from any aim connected with the advancement of material well-being. The pagan forms are represented by actual physical suffering such as throwing oneself under the wheels of a chariot, or living upon a bed of spikes, or allowing the nails of the fingers to grow through the clasped hand. And even in the early forms of the Christian religion we find the saint acquiring merit by living at the top of a pillar or in the desert. But progress in religion is marked by the abandonment of that form of idealism. Catholicism has indeed preserved, the monastery and the nunnery, but most of those institutions now justify their existence by some real social work. And more and more do we apply—and by "we" I include those who subscribe to the dogma—this test to all religious effort and organization: how far does it make the world a better place to live in? I happened recently in Paris to be present at an informal discussion between some French priests touching the question of divorce, and the most suggestive thing about the whole, I thought, was their tendency to justify this or that line taken by the Church by one test: that it made or it did not make for the disintegration of society. And wherever the dogmatic sanction was introduced, I believe it was introduced as an afterthought. And on another occasion a man of religious instincts resented what he regarded as a slighting reference of mine to St. Simon Stylites. He thought to reprove me by pointing out that these lives of austerity were a protest against a condition of society which amounted to social putrefaction. In other words, he justified them by attempting to show that they had a social end; that they made for the betterment of mankind in the widest terms. This line of argument pursued by such a person indicates that the Western man is simply incapable of any other conception. In the long run the final sanction of the religious ideal is the well-being of society. More and more is the Christian conception drifting towards this: Christ came to save this world.

You see, of course, the analogy which I want to draw between religion and political ideals. Like the religious, the earlier forms of political ideals, were divorced from any end of material well-being; they are represented by the personal loyalty of followers to a chief or king. You get a hierarchy of loyalty: the loyalty of the serfs to their lord, their lord to his king. Think of all the gallant effort, the leading of forlorn hopes, the adherence to lost causes, that this personal loyalty has inspired. It is not a mean spectacle; it is a very grand spectacle. And yet the day of that kind of political idealism has passed. And it has passed because no chief who would permanently accept the sacrifice of his subjects or his followers for his mere personal advantage or aggrandizement was worth the sacrifice. Only did he become worth it when he in his person represented some principle or idea embodying the general welfare of his followers, the advantage of the community. So that, in fighting for their king they were fighting for themselves. But this roundabout way of attaining an object lends itself to distortion, and it becomes simpler, and finally necessary, to have political ideals to be centred on the good of the community—that is to say, upon ourselves, upon our interests. Self-sacrifice by the community for the good of the community is a contradiction in terms. If we say that the action taken by a group has in view the interest of that group, the object is self-interest.

It is an old story, of course, for all of you, that complete and universal altruism is self-stultifying. If everyone in a community sacrifices himself for the community he sacrifices the community; he has defeated his own object. But apart from that, one must realise that the modern world has lost its impulse to sterile self-sacrifice; it can no longer believe in a God that demands it, any more than a great democracy could forsake the pursuit of those objects which help to secure the happiness and well-being of millions in order to devote its energies to the dynastic rivalries of royal houses. Such an object, though less selfish, would certainly not be more worthy or more inspiring.

Well, now, I think you will see the application of the illustration which I gave at the beginning of this paper. Ideas do not become less ideal because they have become more closely associated with material welfare. There is a fatal mental confusion in the whole thing. And you may perhaps guess my reason for raising the issue.

In attempting to show that nations in the very essence of the case cannot profit by war, I am met by the retort that men fight not mainly about interest at all. No later than last week the professor of a great English university said that war would go on because men were animated by ideas for which they are prepared to die; and so long as they are thus prepared to give their lives for an ideal possibly quite divorced from any material interest whatsoever, the military contests of States will continue. Another very hostile critic says that it is absurd to suppose that nations fight about "money," and that it would be a very sad and sordid fact if they did. Admiral Mahan says that all my work is vitiated because I assume self-interest on the part of nations in their politics. He says: "To regard the world as governed by self-interest is to live in a non-existent world, a world possessed by an idea much less worthy than those which mankind, to do it bare justice, persistently entertains."

When this criticism comes, by the way, from a supporter of what one may term the orthodox or classic statecraft, one is a little mystified. What were the older accepted interpretations of human motives in the field of international action?

Ideals do not become less ideal because they become more closely associated with material welfare.

The Christian saint who would allow the nails of his fingers to grow through the palm of his clasped hand would excite, not our admiration, but our revolt. More and more is religious effort being subjected to this test: does it make for the improvement of society? If not, it stands condemned. Political ideals will inevitably follow a like development, and will be more and more subjected to a like test. Lecky has summarised the tendency thus: "Interest as distinguished from passion [and if we read for "passion" "unreasoned emotion," the generalization confirms my point] gains a greater empire with advancing civilization."

Progress of this kind here is not marked by a betterment of ideal—a betterment of intention. I have said elsewhere that there was probably as much good intention, as much readiness for self-sacrifice, in the Europe of Simon Stylites as in the Europe of our day; there is perhaps as much to-day in Hindustan or Arabia as in England. But what differentiates the twentieth from the fifth century, or Arabic from British civilisation, is a difference of ideas due to hard mental work; the prime, if not the sole, factor of advance is hard thinking.

That brings us to what I believe to be the real distinction, if any, between the older and the newer Pacifism,—namely, that the older Pacifists appealed to an intuitive unanalyzed ideal, which they did not justify by a process of reasoning, while the New Pacifists attempt to obtain their result by analysis, by showing the how and why of certain facts in human relations, instead of merely holding up an ideal without the process of rationalistic justification.

There are, indeed, favoured persons—those, with a genius for jumping to the right conception —to whom an ideal even unexplained and unjustified by any rational process may immediately appeal. But I do not believe that the average man possesses this special genius, and I maintain that to him, as also to the man already animated by another ideal, you can only appeal by a process of reasoning. Existing beliefs can be undermined only by such a process. Thus, even if finally you replace one unreasoned ideal by another, the process of transition at least will be one of ratiocination. My object is to criticize a very general assumption increasingly favoured in our day: That reason—"logic," as the paragraphist would say—does not affect the conduct of men; that it is hopeless to expect a problem like that of war and peace to be affected by it.

I think the implication is that in the really moving forces of the world reason plays small part; that the strongest impulses to peace, as well as those to war, are non-rational. On the one side you have the Tolstoyan fervour; on the other side the fervour of patriotism, or the determination to right wrong. There is a feeling that the impetus of an intuitive, unreasoned, moral impulse, an ideal emanating from emotion, is greater than that coming from reasoned conviction.

This is in part, perhaps, due to the feeling that the extremist, the intuitionist, is more sincere, and that he gives us a clearer guide in actual policy, because the average man is incapable of theorizing or of splitting hairs; to the feeling that, if you admit war at all, you run the risk of admitting all war; that, if you are for peace, you must not make distinctions between one kind of war and another.

It is with this attitude that I desire to join issue. I believe it involves grave errors of fact, and of psychology, although in so condemning it I do not necessarily exclude intuition as part of the process of the recognition of truth.

It is the service of Bergson—among others—to have shown that many are able to seize a truth by intuition; that some may have an ear for truth, as others for music; that some may see it in a flash of genius, without being able to analyse it or to show us why it is the truth, just as there are natural musicians able to play difficult music by ear. Such in the field of moral truth are the intuitionists, the idealists, the founders of religions, the great moralists, the Tolstoys. But there are others with no ear or with distorted taste making most frightful cacophony. And when one asks how they are to be corrected, these geniuses for moral harmonics stare in wonder. "Why, there is only one way," they say. "Go on playing; the beauty of these harmonies they hear will soon teach them how to play. How did we learn?"

Yes, if we all had the genius for music, it would be enough. But we are not all Tolstoys; and "the glow and fervour" will only communicate itself to those who have the ear, the gift, which most have not. To the workaday world and for workaday folk making their dreadful cacophony you must be able to show in detail, and by humdrum and tiresome analysis, the how and the why of the false notes and the bad time. These have lost their appreciation of harmony, rhythm, melody, and if they are to play in unison at all, and be prevented from making frightful discords, we must teach them the relative values of quavers and crotchets and minims. And without this work of analysis, these arguments and balances of reason, the discords of the great mass never will be corrected.

I do not believe that the man who achieves his conviction as the result of a process of reasoning is less sincere, or has necessarily less fervour, than the man who holds his conviction by intuition—by the inner light. The defender of an old inherited conception is often undoubtedly sincere, but the reformer who has thought himself into new conceptions, modifying and qualifying the old, has generally as great a fervour; and a new movement of ideas like those of the Reformation or the French Revolution, which were in their beginnings purely a matter of argument and discussion, often abstruse, in their development may inflame millions to a high pitch of passion and fervour. While intuition undoubtedly plays its part in determining men's ideas, progress in ideas, the correction of false ideas, is entirely a matter of reasoning. Reason as distinct from emotion is a necessary part of the process of understanding human relationships, and so improving them. While the glow and fervour which go with the possession of an unexamined and unanalyzed ideal have their necessary part in the spiritual life of the world, this mere intuitive inspiration will not and cannot of itself make for improvement, or suffice for a task like the elimination of war. Rational analysis is as necessary a part of that improvement, as it was of that change in the mind of men which gave us freedom from religious oppression, freedom which could never have been achieved unless men had been ready to argue abstruse points of theological difference. This "logic-chopping" of the Reformation, far from having no practical effect on policies and on the conduct of men, had, on the contrary, a revolutionary effect, and that not merely upon their conduct, but upon their psychology; nor can we dogmatically fix any line of demarcation between intuition, or even instinct, and reason. You know that, in the fifteenth century an eminent Catholic said this: "It would be impossible for us Catholics to sit at table with a heretic, because he carries with him a certain odour which is personally intolerable to us." Now, you would have said that here is something purely instinctive and intuitional on the part of the Catholic—unconnected in any way with reasoning. Yet it is curious that when a few men had written books on abstruse points of theology, appealing purely to reason, and when the intellectual ferment so created had done its work, this special odour of the heretic disappeared. For I think the most marvellous thing about that great European transformation of mind which marked the difference between the time of the Massacre of St. Bartholomew and our own is, not that the Catholic should cease massacring the Protestant, and *vice versa*, but that each should cease desiring to do so.

Again the holding of right ideas on essential matters of human conduct, although the result of reasoning, is not dependent upon great learning or a capacity for abstruse argument, but upon the capacity to see simple, visible facts as they are, and to reason simply from them; that the immense majority of us possess this capacity, but have our vision distorted by elaborately constructed spectacles of false theories; and the real work of the dialectician with his learning and logic is to remove those spectacles by destroying the false theories in question. That work of destruction done, the truth stands out of itself clear to ordinary vision.

Let me take a concrete illustration. Between the middle of the seventeenth and eighteenth centuries in Europe, about one hundred thousand persons were condemned to death for witchcraft—condemned by very acute-minded educated men, trained lawyers accustomed to sift evidence. Moreover, many of these men had made a close study of the "science" of witchcraft, and thoroughly believed in it. There were, nevertheless, a few men much earlier than this—Montaigne was one—who saw that this "science" was just learned rubbish; and one of them, who himself saw quite clearly the real character of witchcraft, expressed this opinion: "The bulk of mankind will always believe in witchcraft. When you get highly educated and exceptional men believing it, what possible hope is there of the average man, with his loose notions of evidence and probability, ever coming to see its errors? Not one brain in a million is capable of the learning and clearness of view necessary to refute these misconceptions."

Doubtless, if any one of us here had attempted to argue with one of those eighteenth-century judges, we should have been hopelessly beaten. Yet if you put this question to an ordinary school boy: "Do you regard it as likely that an old woman could cause a storm at sea and make a Scotch King seasick?" He would reply immediately and dogmatically: "No, it isn't likely."

Why is he thus able to dogmatize? He has not studied the heavy tomes familiar to the eighteenth-century judges. But he has formed the habit of judging natural phenomena straight, of seeing facts just simply as they are; of drawing the simplest and easiest conclusions from them with a mind untwisted by hypotheses, uninfluenced by the theories of goblins and portents which weighed upon the intelligence of the seventeenth century. Without the prepossessions of such theories, he interprets phenomena directly and not through the spectacles which those theories constituted. Owing to the turn given to his mind by the attitude of those about him towards external things, he unconsciously adopts the inductive method of reasoning, a method which men are sometimes led to abandon during whole millenniums.

That is the story of most advances in human ideas—politics, religion, medicine, sociology. Advance is achieved by the destruction of elaborate theorems with which the past has covered easily perceptible facts. Once destroy that overgrowth, and the right idea emerges. Parenthetically, you will realize that the destruction of false theories was by no means a simple matter; that the work demanded vast learning, infinite toil, superhuman patience. If we are to do this necessary work of destruction, we cannot afford to dismiss as logic-chopping and hair-splitting the analysis of those theories upon which false conceptions are built. Men are governed by theories—often false theories—and any approach to their reason must be by reason. You cannot cure false thinking by more false thinking. What often looks like complication of thought is really its simplification.

I should like just to give a hint of the way in which, in the field of international politics, the recognition of simple, obvious facts—a recognition calling for no special knowledge, but possible on the data available to anyone of ordinary intelligence—is prevented by old theories, just as the improbability of an old woman causing a storm at sea was hidden from the learned judge who had been brought up in a mental atmosphere of witches and goblins.

Take the commonest assumptions connected with war and peace, and test them in the light, not of unknown or disputed facts, but of the undisputed facts of common knowledge. Here is Mr. Churchill, who lays it down as an axiom that the way for nations to preserve peace is "to be so strong that victory in the event of war is certain." Now, as in war there are two parties, he has propounded, as an axiom, a physical absurdity. The parties cannot apply it, since each cannot be stronger than the other.

Here is Lord Roberts, who says that British over-sea trade depends upon her naval superiority; that if a foreign nation became stronger at sea it would not tolerate her trade competition. Yet the trade competition of Germany has grown and developed during the period in which she was Great Britain's inferior at sea, and she has been unable to check that competition by her naval superiority. The statesmen of Europe assume as an axiom that to take territory is to take wealth—for a nation to enrich itself. And yet the richest peoples are those of the very smallest nations. We are told that Germany must fight England because she is hungry—she must have the wheat of Canada and the wool of Australia. She can have them now by paying for them; and if she conquered those countries she would still have to pay for them in the same way. The British talk and think of themselves as the "owners" of Canada—as having rights of proprietorship over eight million people of their own race—whereas a moment's reflection shows that they have no such rights at all. The militarists, who talk of the discipline of war and the dangers of peace appeal for more armaments in order to preserve peace and keep us from war. We talk of the survival of the fittest by war, when the evident process of war is to kill off the more fit and to insure the survival of the less fit. Our public men make our flesh creep by talking knowingly of the "intentions" of a nation of sixty-five million people; what they will do five, ten, or fifteen years hence; when we should laugh at them if they professed to know the intentions of their own countrymen—even at the next General Election.

Now, we find, in all these cases, precisely what we found in the case of the learned seventeenth-century judges who justified witchcraft. The pundits, learned men defending the old conceptions, will not allow us to judge by the ordinary evidence of our senses, to give the natural interpretation to evident facts. We must see them through the old spectacles. Thus, because Roman law and terminology play so large a part in forming our mental pictures—and to the Roman State a province was really something owned and exploited for a ruling caste, the product of the mines and the tribute of the taxes actually going to rulers in Rome—we still think of conquest as the acquisition of wealth for the conquering State;

whereas, of course, it is merely the enlargement of the area of administration, and to suppose that annexation enriches the conquering state is as though one should assume that the State of New York would enrich New Yorkers by conquering Maine. Thus it comes that an educated man—the professor of a great university—asked in a discussion: "If conquest does not enrich the conqueror, why should we not give away Canada?" I asked him how he proposed to "give away" eight million Canadians, and asked him also if he would enumerate what were the functions of "ownership" that Britain was now able to exercise over those eight millions of people.

In the same way we have inherited the terminology and the mental pictures of feudal struggles, of the time when a State was a person, a family; and we talk of the competition of German trade as though Germany were an economic unit, a business house. There is, of course, no such thing, properly speaking, as German trade in the international field. We talk of hating or of having a friendship for Germany or "Germans"—sixty-four millions of men, women, and children, whom we have never seen, and in the nature of things never can see; who do not, and cannot, come into personal contact with us; whose personal characters and idiosyncrasies can no more affect us than those of the inhabitants of Baluchistan or Thibet, or, for that matter, of Mars. We utterly fail to realize that we are talking of an abstraction

—we might as well talk about loving or hating the Tropic of Capricorn.

Nor is it true that the qualifications and distinctions demanded by reasoning make for confusion of thought or necessarily reduce a whole-souled homogeneous doctrine to hair-splitting expediences; nor that if we admit the right of self-defence we give a justification to any war, all war, since a nation can always argue itself into the belief that it is the aggrieved or attacked party. Moncure Conway made a distinction between defensive war which he justified, and war of aggression, which he did not. This said Mr. Nevinson, who preceded me in these lectures, is equivalent to justifying all war. Yet so little was that the case in Conway's mind that he condemned even the War of Independence and the War of the Union. The admission that force may rightly be resisted in no way blinded him to the truth that military defence is generally the worst kind of defence; that it is generally clumsy, ineffective, futile, and stupid; that the instinct to fly to arms in revenge for wrong is as often dictated by an appetite for violent action as by the desire to right a wrong; and that the indulgence of this appetite, the luxury of temper, is often a betrayal of the cause of justice by the submission of that cause to the hazards of physical force.

I want you to follow with me the distinction which I believe was in Conway's mind, because I don't believe we can properly state the case against force until we have that distinction clear. Conway's point was that defence is not war; I want to show that this was not an attempt to alter things by altering names. It was an attempt to distinguish between the name and the thing; to distinguish between two very different things which are commonly confused.

How shall we define war? Surely, as the use of physical coercion for the purpose of imposing the will of one group upon another, and, to the extent to which force is operative, dispensing with the need for understanding common interest, and for free agreement. It is the rule of coercion, eliminating consent, reason and co-operation in the relationship of the two parties involved.

Now, I like to think that Conway saw that defence, the resistance to the employment of military force against you, was not war as I have defined it, but the negation of war—the effort necessary to prevent force, your enemy's force, replacing the common reason of both.

Let us assume two parties to this discussion. On the one side you have those who do not believe that force should enter into human relations, who believe that it should be excluded; and on the other side you have those who believe that force must be the ultimate appeal, the ultimate fact, or in human affairs. If you belong to the first party (to which I claim to belong), you must, says Mr. Nevinson, be a non-resister, which Conway was not. He, Conway, approved self-defence; therefore we are to conclude that he belongs to the force party, or that he is inconsistent.

I believe that this is simply a confusion of thought due largely, as I have said, to the inadequacy of our language.

What is the position? I say that a difference between two parties should not be settled by physical force. Therefore, I am told, if someone uses physical force against me, I should submit—thus allowing the matter to be settled by physical force. But that is precisely the solution to which my principles are opposed. How, therefore, can I approve it? If I am true to my principle, I should say to a person attacked: "Since you do not believe that this matter should be settled by coercion, try and prevent it being settled in that way—that is to say, resist. Neutralize the force of the other party by equivalent force. But, having so neutralized it, see that you do not use coercion to settle the matter in your favour."

Let me put it in another way; and, if in these illustrations I am guilty of damnable iteration, I will beg you to consider that this is a matter in which infinite confusion exists, and even the simplest illustrations seem to mislead. Suppose I declare to one of you that you owe me money. You deny it. I say: "Well, I believe that I am right, and, as I am the stronger party, I am going to take it." I attack you; you resist and succeed in disarming me. You then say: "I have neutralized your force by my own. I have taken your arm from you. I will now hear what you have to say as to why I should pay you money. The justice of the case is going to settle this matter, not force."

So far you would be a pacifist. If, however, you said: "Since you have no means of compelling this payment, I am not going to worry as to whether I owe you money or not"—then you would be a militarist, because you would be using your force, though passively, to settle the matter to your advantage, irrespective of right. Still more, if you said: "Since preponderant force is the final judgment; since it is the law of life that the strong eats up the weak; and since the preponderant power has passed from you to me, I am now going to see that you pay me money"—would you be a militarist.

Assume, however, that you are not sufficiently strong to resist me, and that you call in the policeman. What is his *rôle?* It is to prevent me from using coercion against you. He says: "I will see that this matter is not settled by force. We will have the judge sift it out; and reason, the best reason that we can obtain, shall settle it, not force. We are here to prevent a settlement by force."

In every civilized country the basis of the relationship on which the community rests is this: no individual is allowed to settle his differences with another by coercion. But does this mean that, if one threatens to take my purse, I am not allowed to use force to prevent such coercion? That, if he threatens to kill me, I am not to defend myself, because the "individual citizens are not allowed to settle their differences by force"? It is *because* of that, *because* the act of self-defence is an attempt to prevent the settlement of a difference by force, that the law justifies it.

But the law would not justify me if, having disarmed my opponent, having neutralized his force by my own and re-established the social equilibrium, I immediately proceeded to upset it by asking him for his purse on pain of murder. I should then be settling the matter by force—I should then have ceased to be a pacifist, (or perhaps should I say "civilist"?) and have become a militarist.

That is the difference between the two conceptions. The militarist says: "Force alone can settle these matters; it is the final appeal; therefore fight it out. Let the best man win. When you have preponderant strength, impose your view. Force the other man to your will, not because it is right, but because you are able to do so." This is the "excellent policy" which Lord Roberts attributes to Germany and approves.

We say, of course; "To fight it out settles nothing, since it is not a question of who is stronger, but of whose view is right; and, as that is not always easy to establish, it is of the utmost importance in the interest of all parties, in the long run, to keep force out of it."

You will say: "This is logic-chopping. The

final instrument used in all these matters is force; in the last resort you would use the army to enforce the decisions of the Court."

But my whole point is that you are using force for the prevention of individual coercion, for the neutralization of force, not for the settlement of the matter. Trial by battle was settlement by force.

Indeed, in this country at least, the final appeal between the citizens is not force, because we determine *how* the army shall be used by reason, by Parliament, by the vote. The army acts as the voter directs, not the voter as the army directs. In Venezuela or in Turkey it is different, and it is precisely that difference which distinguishes our civilization from theirs.

If we are in disagreement about a law, we do not fight it out; we argue it out and settle it by ballot, not bullets. We have agreed to decide by the result of the vote. Where does force come in?

Now, of course, in Venezuela or Turkey or Mexico, force, the armies of the rival Presidents, *would* settle it. Venezuelan society is really based on the militarist principle, the principle of force; ours is really based upon the civilist, as opposed to the militarist principle.

At the time of the discussion of the Parliament Act a correspondent of one of the papers asked this question: "When the House of Lords has been abolished and the House of Commons is supreme, what is to prevent the Radical majority from suspending the Septennial Act, voting themselves members for life with a thousand a year apiece, and making themselves dictators of Great Britain?"

Well, what is there, since they, Parliament, control the army and the navy, and thus can overbear all the nation? If you say that the army and navy are mainly Conservative, and would not obey a Liberal Government, then what is to prevent a Conservative Government from doing it? What, in other words, is to prevent each side using force when it finds itself in possession, to install itself definitely in power until dispossessed by rival force, just as is done in Nicaragua or Mexico? Nothing in this world save the mutual agreement of the two parties concerned that the differences between them shall not be settled in that way—an agreement based on mutual recognition that that is a miserably poor way to settle it, that force, indeed, cannot "settle it" at all—cannot decide what is in the best interests of the parties concerned, it can only decide which of them is stronger.

What does it mean when we hear of a country that it has had forty revolutions in fifty years? It means that the rival parties have been "settling" their differences by force, that a President or party in power is not prepared to yield to votes, only to coercion. What does it mean when the President or party quietly steps down from power when outvoted but that they have decided to abide by votes, and not to introduce the element of force?

It is simply untrue to say that the Insurance Bill has become law because Mr. Asquith had the army behind him; for, if he had to enforce it with the army, it would not have become law. Nor does Mr. Asquith hold office because he can wield armed force; it is a matter of arrangement and consent, and, incidentally, society progresses to the degree to which we can eliminate the factor of force in the settlement of differences between us; and I will venture to assert that this is the Law of Progress—the Elimination of Physical Force. For where we keep force out of it we are obliged to use our reason, to find what is best, and to discover the basis of permanent settlement.

Let me add this. We only drop the use of force when it becomes difficult of use or ineffective, and part of the work of rendering it difficult and ineffective is resistance to it. Resistance is a necessary part of achieving the general recognition of the futility of force. Of course, it is not the only part—I think it soon becomes the least important part of the process of such recognition. But in the earlier stage, when we are able to use force—obviously, effectively, and immediately to impose our view—we do not trouble to find a reasoned settlement , or, rather should I say, we are not compelled to find a reasoned settlement. Professor Giddings has put it a little obscurely, thus:

"So long as we can confidently act, we do not argue; but when we face conditions abounding in uncertainty or when we are confronted by alternative possibilities, we first hesitate, then feel our way, then guess, and at length venture to reason. Reasoning, accordingly, is that action of the mind to which we resort when the possibilities before us and about us are distributed substantially according to the law of chance occurrence or, as the mathematician would say, in accordance with "the normal curve" of random frequency. The moment the curve is obviously skewed, we decide; if it is obviously skewed from the beginning, by bias or interest, by prejudice, authority, or coercion, our reasoning is futile or imperfect. So, in the State, if any interest or coalition of interests is dominant, and can act promptly, it rules by absolutist methods. Whether it is benevolent or cruel, it wastes neither time nor resources upon government by discussion. But if interests are innumerable, and so distributed as to offset one another, and if no great bias or overweighting anywhere appears, government by discussion inevitably arises. The interests can get together only if they talk. If power shall be able to dictate, it will also rule, and the appeal to reason will be vain."

Now, it is obvious that the character of any given community is determined by the character of the ideas of the individuals who compose it. The difference between the Turk—or, for that matter, the Zulu—and ourselves is not a difference of physical force or raw materials of nature (they have splendid physique, a soil and climate as good as our own); the difference is one of ideas. The history of civilization is the history of the development of ideas. It is a truism; but one of those truisms we are always forgetting. And the development of ideas is correlated to the decline of physical force in the way I have just indicated. That is to say, where physical force is made inoperative by neutralization, you get the operation of the alternative factor, which is reason and adjustment. And that is the case against physical force.

It is hardly necessary to point out that, in order to maintain the state of balance or equilibrium in which reason works, it is by no means necessary to meet every exhibition of physical force by a similar exhibition. Force is often so futile and ineffective as not seriously to influence the balance. The growing recognition of its futility and mischief on the one hand, and on the other the growing realization of the superiority of reason, prevents the introduction of the element of force, as we have seen, in the case of Governments that grow from the Venezuelan to the English type. For, of course, an equilibrium can as well be maintained with nothing in either scale as with millions of tons of dangerously explosive material in both.

If you still deem that the growing rationalization of conceptions can work little in the domain of international politics because of the immense strength of the intuitive unreasoned impulses we associate with patriotism, I would call your attention again to this point.

All the improvement in human thought shown by the period of the Reformation—that immense development in the mind of Europe which enables Catholics and Protestants to live in complete peace, when less than three centuries ago the differences between them were the cause of wars and cruelties and abominations more vile and monstrous even than those which occur in our political quarrels; the abolition of witchcraft, of judicial torture, of barbaric criminal codes, of the Inquisition, of the duel—all this development has its root in reason, in argument, in discussion. All the force of intuition was on the side of the retention of these things. The old Inquisitor was quite sure that he was right; the Catholic sure that on the night of St. Bartholomew "God would recognize His own." Those old impulses were transformed and those old evils destroyed by reason. As I have said, the odour of the heretic disappeared when certain books had been written and certain somewhat abstruse points of theology discussed.

It is noteworthy, by the way, that the factors which favoured the retention of the right of Governments to dictate religious belief were infinitely stronger than those which now favour the retention of force for the imposition of the ideals of one political group upon another. And I would ask those who believe that, while war may have lost its economic advantage, it must be a permanent element in the settlement of the moral differences of men, to think for one moment of the factors which stood in the way of the abandonment of the use of force by Governments and by one religious group against another in the matter of religious belief. On the one hand you had priestly authority, with all the prestige of historical right and the possession of physical power in its most imposing form, the means of education, still in its hands; Government authority extending to all sorts of details of life to which it no longer extends; immense vested interests outside government; and finally the case for the imposition of dogma by authority a strong one, and still supported by popular passion. And on the other hand you had as yet poor and feeble instruments of mere opinion—the printed book still a rarity, the Press non-existent, communication between men still rudimentary, worse even than it had been two thousand years previously. And yet, despite these immense handicaps upon the growth of opinion and intellectual ferment as against physical force, it was impossible for a new idea to find life in Geneva or Rome, or Edinburgh or London, without quickly crossing and affecting all the other centres, and not merely making headway against entrenched authority, but so quickly breaking up the religious homogeneity of States that not only were Governments obliged to abandon the use of force in religious matters as against their subjects, but religious wars between nations became impossible, for the double reason that a nation no longer expressed a single religious belief (you had the anomaly of a Protestant Sweden fighting in alliance with a Catholic France), and that the power of opinion had become stronger than the power of physical force—because, in other words, the limits of military force were more and more receding.

But if the use of force was ineffective against the spiritual possessions of man when the arms to be used in their defence were so poor and rudimentary, how could a Government hope to crush out by physical coercion to-day such things as a nation's language, law, literature, morals, ideals, when it possesses such means of defence as are provided in security of tenure of material possessions, a cheap literature, a popular Press, a cheap and secret postal system, and all the other means of rapid and perfected intercommunication?

You will notice that I have spoken throughout not of the *defence* of a national ideal by arms, but of its attack; if you have to defend your ideal it is because someone attacks it, and without attack your defence would not be called for.

If you are compelled to prevent someone using force as against your nationality, it is because he believes that by the use of that force he can destroy or change it. If he thought that the use of force would be ineffective to that end he would not employ it.

I have attempted to show elsewhere that the abandonment of war for material ends depends upon a general realization of its futility for accomplishing those ends. In like manner does the abandonment of war for moral or ideal ends depend upon the general realization of the growing futility of such means for those ends also.

We are sometimes told that it is the spirit of nationality—the desire to be of your place and locality—that makes war. That is not so. It is the desire of other men that you shall not be of your place and locality, of your habits and traditions, but of theirs. Not the desire of nationality, but the desire to destroy nationality is what makes the wars of nationality. If the Germans did not think that the retention of distinctive nationality by Poles and Alsatians might hamper them in the art of war, hamper them in the imposition of force on some other groups, there would be no attempt to crush out this special possession of the Poles and Alsatians. It is the belief in force and a preference for settling things by force instead of by agreement that threatens or destroys nationality. And I have given an indication of the fact that it is not merely war, but the preparation for war, implying as it does great homogeneity in States and centralized bureaucratic control, which is to-day the great enemy of nationality. Before this tendency to centralization which military necessity sets up much that gives colour and charm to European life is disappearing. And yet we are told that it is the Pacifists who are the enemy of nationality, and we are led to believe that in some way the war system in Europe stands for the preservation of nationality!

The practical question, therefore, is this: Are the

great moral divisions of the great world such that we are likely to find them expressed in one national ideal as against another national ideal? In actual politics this question can never be answered in the affirmative. In the latent conflicts between Britain and Germany, what is the moral ideal impelling the assumed aggression of Germany? If ends which cannot be expressed in terms of tangible advantage—extending trade and territory and the rest—are not at the bottom of that prospective aggression, what are the moral motives behind it? I have, indeed, seen it suggested that Germany will enter upon a crusade to subdue Britain in the interests of autocracy in Europe; and such arguments used to be much commoner when Russia was the enemy instead of Germany.

The idea that the mere destruction of a rival fleet or army is equivalent to the "suppression" of a rival nation's moral influence, the same loose use of words that we find in the economic sphere. The conception of international trade competition as the conflict of rival military units, the idea that the military defeat of Germany would imply the removal of her industrial competition, overlooks completely the fact that the hands and brains of sixty-five millions engaged in producing and manufacturing, and buying and selling, would exist after the destruction of the German fleet as before, and that no essential economic fact would be altered by Germany's military defeat. So, exactly in the same way, those who imagine that the moral and intellectual possessions of a people can be taken from them by military force have simply not examined the limits of that force in our time. Even though Germany *did* "vanquish" Britain, some fifty-five or sixty millions of English-speaking people—some one hundred and fifty millions if you include the United States—would remain with their own laws, literature, political traditions just as before and they would remain as great an intellectual and moral force in the world as ever. Even though Germany were so completely successful as to be able to effect the incorporation of Britain into her Empire she would then necessarily incorporate the very elements which it was the object of the war to prevent from touching her Empire; a war undertaken for the purpose of destroying anti-autocratic elements would have resulted in introducing into the new German Empire an immensely strong element of anti-autocratic ferment. All experience shows these moral and spiritual elements to be impossible of destruction, even where the disproportion of power in favour of the conqueror is overwhelming, as in the case of Germany in her Polish and Alsatian provinces. The characteristic fact in the history of the relationship of the Empire to the Poles and to the inhabitants of Alsace-Lorraine is that the efforts towards Germanizing have failed after half a century of struggle in the one case and more in the other. Attempts are now being made by Germany to get rid of these political sores which by such palliatives as autonomous government—an admission that the policy of conquest has failed even in those microscopic cases.*

And if you now say that, of course, no such effort of incorporation would in the case of Britain be made, then we are forced to the conclusion that British political philosophy and ideas remain as part of the intellectual ferment of the world, and would go on unchecked.

I have attempted to indicate elsewhere the moral results of the intangibility of material wealth in the modern world, and that confiscation of private property on a large scale by a conqueror in our day is impossible. Canada or Australia after German conquest—if we could imagine such a thing possible—would necessarily remain pretty much the same Canada or Australia as before. Since you cannot turn the business man out of his business and the farmer out of his farm, since they are thus secure in the means of livelihood for their families, they are in a position to resist all effort at Germanization. They will not send their children to the German school, nor write their letters in German, nor say their prayers therein; and, given all the factors of the case, it would be a physical

* On the occasion of the Zabern affair, the German Chancellor said in the Reichstag: "It is evident that we cannot make North German Prussians of these South German Alsatians." And in a letter written just previously to Professor Lamprecht of Leipzig, he said: "Some of the ideas of certain of our German parties as to what military force can accomplish are simply childish in their naïveté."

impossibility for Germany to make them do so, conquest or no conquest. It was not always so, but it is so to-day.

That is why I have spoken of military force as irrelevant in the spiritual conflicts of men. Even assuming that moral differences did coincide with the political grouping, which, of course, they do not, even then the obvious limits of military force in the modern world are such that it can have no real bearing upon the enforcement of a moral ideal.

In dealing with the economic case I have attempted to show that the modern intangibility of wealth, arising from the credit system, is due to a condition of interdependence between individuals of different groups, which interdependence in its turn has arisen from the international division of labour. Lancashire divides the work of cotton production with Louisiana, and cannot do its own share of production without the co-operation of that foreign State. But an exactly similar condition of intellectual interdependence has arisen from the fact that the intellectual divisions of mankind as well as their material and economic activities now cut athwart political frontiers. The questions which really divide men—opposing conceptions of government and society, Socialism as against individualism, etc.—are not French or German or British conceptions, but are ideas common to all these nations. Germany is more socialistic in the general sense than is Britain; Britain is more democratic; it is not British Parliamentarism that worries the German Government, but German Social Democracy. For Germany to "destroy" Britain would not solve the problem. There could be no such event as anti-Socialist Germany fighting a Socialist Britain. The armies of the nations could not embody the rival ideas, the growth of these ideas having entirely disregarded political grouping. We have here, therefore, all the factors which led to the abandonment of military force between religious groups in Europe three or four centuries ago. Indeed, the factors which favoured the retention of the right of Governments to dictate religious belief were infinitely stronger than those which now favour the retention of force for the imposition of the ideals of one political group upon another.

War between the religious groups was brought to an end by saner conceptions concerning the relation of physical coercion to religious opinion—saner conceptions due to the discussions which were the outcome of the Reformation. A similar process will destroy political wars.

The final entrenchment of our critics is, that the general realization, by European opinion, of the new facts of life which make war morally and materially futile cannot be expected; that the nations are impervious to argument, the public impervious to instruction. Well, the facts I have cited show it not to be true. But if it were true, what should we do? Should we assume that because men do not readily see the facts, therefore we should not endeavour to ascertain them; that, because men are, in part, guided by temper and passion, we should not try any more to find the truth in these matters? Such a conclusion would involve a fatalism which is and must be alien to the Western World. We *do* and *must* reason and talk about these things with more or less of wisdom; we all assume that men will listen to reason and are not indifferent to the truth when it is shown them. The fact that preachers preach, that men produce books and write in newspapers—implies that they all believe that in the end their preaching and talking and writing and reasoning will do something to modify human conduct.

And, in the end, that belief will be justified. What we call public opinion does not descend upon us from the outside, is not something outside our acts and volition, but the reflection of those acts; it is not made for us, we make it. That we are the instruments of our own salvation, that, without the act of the individual there can be no salvation, is a truth that has the sanction alike of economics, of morals, and of religion. And the contrary view—that nothing that we can do will affect our destiny—is one that the Western World and its religion have rejected. For, to the degree to which it is accepted, it involves stagnation and decline. If it were true, it would take, from the finer activities of life, all that gives dignity to human society, since it would make of men the blind puppets of the brute forces of nature; it would imply the decay and death of the human soul, of the better things for which men live.

III

THE INFLUENCE OF CREDIT UPON INTERNATIONAL RELATIONS

(A Lecture delivered before the Institute of Bankers of Great Britain, January 17, 1912)

I HAVE so often submitted this matter to the criticism of people having no special equipment for understanding the more fundamental forces with which it is concerned, that the pleasure I have in laying it before those who possess such special equipment is, I imagine, difficult for you to realise.

Not that I am going to deal with any abstract points of banking theory or practice, concerning which I have no particular competence; I would not come here with the presumption of being able to teach you anything about the details of your own work. But rather do I want to call your attention, interrogatively, to certain large social and economic reactions of banking as a whole—certain general effects of a condition which has grown up, to some extent unnoticed, perhaps, even by those responsible for it. To produce this condition was not the object of your work, but it is one of its results, and as I think you will agree, not the least important. And if I can establish this connection, you at least will be able to realize the force and sweep of the factors at work.

The title of this address might suggest to you, perhaps, that I was going to deal with a phase of the connection between banking and international relations, of which we have heard a great deal of late—I mean the alleged direct interference of eminent financiers, or groups of financiers, with the negotiations between European Governments. Well, that is not the phase with which I intend to deal, except that in a word or two, I shall try to reduce it to its right proportions. Among those who deal with international affairs, you will find a type of writer, with a taste presumably for the melodramatic, who would have us believe that, behind every diplomatic difference and every international settlement stands what he is apt to call "the sinister figure of the international financier." According to this view, nations and peoples are mere pawns in the hands of those who constitute that mysterious entity "the money power." War is, or is not declared, we are given to understand, because "the money power" wants it, or it does not want it. You are aware, of course, of the somewhat childish confusion between the personal power or influence of a merchant or financier and the forces of which he may be a trustee, which makes such a picture, for the most part, a caricature. Separate even the most powerful of these "sinister figures" from the interests or the economic forces, of which for the moment he may be the representative, and he is reduced to practical impotence.

The Bank Court may make the Bank-rate (because that is not always a commercial reality), but it cannot make—at most it can but register—the market rate. A Court of Law does not make the guilt of a prisoner. We talk commonly of an assize court holding in its hands the issues of life and death. It is dramatic, but not true, except in a very narrow sense. The Court cannot hang a man plainly innocent for stealing a pennyworth of corn, although it could have done so two or three generations ago. It cannot flagrantly flout the law of evidence, or certain customs and tradition; it is, in fact, the expression of forces outside its control. In the same way, when we talk of a group of financiers bringing a war to a close by stopping supplies, as though it were the personal fiat of the individuals or corporations involved, what we really mean is that the credit of the particular Power, to which supplies have been refused, is no longer sound—an economic fact quite outside the control of the bankers. Had its credit remained sound, the nation in question could, by bettering the terms, have raised the money elsewhere.

I read the other day in a serious review, that in the recent Franco-German rivalry, the diplomats had become the mere mouthpieces of the financiers, the latter being able by their influence to decree the course of events—to render it impossible or possible, as they desired, for one or the other side to declare war—the truth being, of course, that diplomats and financiers alike were both equally impotent in the face of a financial situation due to causes and events stretching over a generation. For twenty or thirty years, Germany had been a developing and borrowing nation, and France a saving and lending nation, a difference due to economic, moral, religious, and racial forces, over which the financiers have no more control than they have over the tides of the sea. And the French Government has, within the last few weeks, had a potent lesson, showing the very narrow limits within which either governments or financiers can control or set at naught the impersonal economic forces of the modern world. They have learned that, thanks to processes familiar to you, which I shall touch on in some detail in a minute to illustrate certain secondary results, it has become impossible to impose more than a momentary check upon French money going to the help of German credit, if the intricate economic needs based on the interdependence of the civilized world call for it.

In politics, as in business, art, literature, philosophy, religion, or medicine, you get men of capacity, playing, by virtue of the greater skill with which they apply their gifts, whether moral or intellectual, to material circumstances, a larger *rôle* than others in the same sphere of activity; but to pretend that organized finance aims in any special sense at monopolizing or controlling political power is, so far as one can generalize at all in the matter, to turn facts upside down. For the most part, it is not the banker who wants to interfere with politics, it is the politician who wants to interfere with banking: all that the banker generally asks of politics is to be left alone. Again and again, in the history of banking, from the days that Kings, as a matter of course, debased coinage to their personal profit, so that bankers were obliged to resort to the expedient of an imaginary coin, do we find, especially in the history of Continental banking, that pressure has been brought upon bankers to compel them against their judgment to make their business serve some political end of the Government. Again and again, do we find illicit political pressure put upon them to use funds, entrusted to them, for purposes which such trust did not imply. I think it is Courtois, in his "History of Banking in France," who declares that the desperate financial disasters which marked the history of France for the best part of a century were due practically to one cause, and to one cause only: the illicit power exercised by the Government over banks, compelling them against their judgment to make advances to the Government, or to favour this or that political scheme which happened to fit in with the political needs of the moment. He declares that had the bankers been allowed to carry on their business uninterfered with, like most other business men, an infinity of suffering and poverty would have been spared to the country. And the strength of this feeling, against being mixed up with politics or having any connection with the State, felt by Continental financiers may be judged by the vehemence of the language used in this respect by the founders of the Bank of France.

To this day, the connection of the great credit institutions of the Continent with their respective governments is a very much closer connection than that which exists between the banks and the government in this country. The Syndicat des Agents de Change in France, for instance, cannot, or, at least, does not, authorize the official quotation of a security on the Paris Bourse without the express sanction of the Government: and although such control has never received the authority of an Act of Parliament, the great French credit institutions do not facilitate the issue of any large foreign government loan in France unless it has received the approval of their Government. Indeed, it is well known that in the issue of such loans, they are guided to no small extent by the political necessities of the Government. In the case of Germany, political control, though not operating in quite the same way, is still more direct. Bismarck, on more than one occasion, practically compelled banks to operate on the market at his dictation, in order that he might exercise diplomatic pressure on a foreign Government. Whether it is desirable that a bank should be compelled to carry on its business, not solely with a view to its security and prosperity and in the interests of its clients, but also with a view to purely political purposes, is a question on which I think you would have very grave doubts, especially since, as I think I shall be able to make plain to you before I have done, the political object almost always miscarries and the interference has had, both with France and Germany, in every single important case shown by the history of the last forty years, effects the exact contrary to those aimed at by the respective Governments.

It is not therefore of this alleged personal control of policy by great financial interests, a subject upon which a vast deal of nonsense has been written owing to the misconception which I have sought to explain, that I want to treat, but the influence of banking operating in quite another way: by the unnoticed impersonal forces which the ordinary weekday, humdrum work of banking has called into existence; the cumulative outcome of those numberless everyday operations that take place almost completely outside the control of governments or financiers: often unknown to them; often in spite of them; representing forces far too strong and far too elusive for such control; so much a part of the warp and woof of the ordinary life of the world that they are rapidly and surely weaving society into one indissoluble whole. I want to treat of banking as a permanent and integral part of the great social organism—the outcome of functions which are as vital, as unconscious, and as uncontrollable as respiration, or digestion in the case of an animal organism.

I should here, perhaps, anticipate a *caveat* that you might enter touching this illustration or analogy, which, like all illustrations and analogies, is liable to misuse. If these forces, you may argue, are so powerful as to offset the force of political combinations, why are we worrying about the matter at all? We have only to let the politicians do their worst. Such a conclusion would not be justified. While the vital processes of an organism—respiration, digestion, blood-circulation—are unconscious and uncontrollable, the life of the whole thing may depend upon whether conscious volition is so used as to enable it to carry on those processes favourably, and the more that the organism grows in vitality by adaptation to its environment, the more important does the factor of conscious volition, which, in the case of man, means his intelligence, become. A man cannot control his breathing, but he can bring it to a stop by committing suicide, or damage it by catching bronchitis from sitting in a draught; he cannot control his digestion, but he can avoid indigestion by refraining from poisonous foods. If you catch cold or take poison, you are not master of the fact as to whether you will die, your conscious volition cannot control it—unless you are a Christian Scientist, and Christian Science has not yet been applied to banking. But you *are* master of the fact as to whether you will sit in a draught or swallow horribly-tasting things, and you are master of that fact, thanks to the development of sensory nerves. In the absence of these the organism would die. If we can imagine an animal that did not feel hunger or cold or the bad taste of poisons, it would very soon be wiped out. It would have nothing to guide it in its adaptation to its environment, none of the acute promptings which result in placing it in the most favourable conditions to allow the unconscious and uncontrollable processes to be carried on.

Now, credit is performing, among other functions, this immense service to the economic and social organism; it is providing it with sensory nerves, by which damage to any part or to any function can be felt, and, thanks to such feeling, avoided.

By banking, I mean all that the word can legitimately imply—the whole process of the systematic organisation of credit. And I think I can show you that banking, in this large sense, thanks to the evolution and development of those sensory nerves, is bound to bring about not merely a considerable, but a revolutionary, change in the general conduct of the organism which we call human society—bringing vividly to its consciousness certain errors in conduct, errors which become increasingly painful by reason precisely of the developments of its nervous system.

This sensitiveness is shown, of course, mainly

where the organism works with most difficulty—in the relationship between nations. And I believe that in the never-ending struggle which every nation carries on, in the attempt to adapt itself to environment, it is bound to discard more and more certain habits which have marked it in the less developed stage.

What are the principles which have dictated the general conduct of nations the one to the other in the past—not merely in Europe, but in Christendom; and which have created what we call the European situation, with its competition of armaments and all its recurrent dangers?

There is no occasion to use exaggerated language about that situation and its dangers; the one point upon which men of all opinions are agreed is that the situation is very dangerous indeed. Your big navy man, your advocate of universal military service, justifies his demands for an enormous expenditure of money and energy by reference to our ever-increasing danger. If that danger did not exist, these enormous sacrifices, which he demands, would not be justified. And those of us who are not concerned with politics, and take no side on the question, the business world, for instance, of which this city is the centre, know that war would bring damage, of which no man can foretell the limit.

What sets up this situation, turns the world in this way into a volcano, ever threatening eruption? The necessity for defence? But that implies that someone may attack—that someone has a motive for attack; and, if the danger is as imminent as these vast preparations would suggest, it means that such a motive must be a strong one. It is the assumption that this strong motive does exist which creates the whole situation. To say that the likelihood of being attacked depends upon the likelihood of someone making the attack is, of course, to utter a truism, and that leads us to ask what is the impelling motive, material or moral, making this attack as probable as we allege.

Those whose special competence is the philosophy of statecraft, from Aristotle and Plato, passing by Machiavelli and Clausewitz down to Mr. Roosevelt and the German Emperor, or, for that matter, to Mr. Blatchford, have never for a moment disguised their opinion that this motive does exist. It forms the basic premise of the whole science of international relationship as we now know it: "war is a part of policy," in Clausewitz's phrase. Since nations must struggle one with the other for their "place in the sun," the race is to the strong militarily: the strong are able to benefit themselves at the expense of the weak, and a nation must be strong militarily and use its force, or threaten to use its force, to ensure an advantageous situation in the world. And this conception is justified on moral grounds by an appeal to the analogies of evolution, and we are told that its final justification is to be found in the fact that such struggle ensures the survival of the fittest. It is the great struggle for life which is coterminous with the whole of organic existence.

What we may properly call these foundations of European statecraft have been well stated by two writers of acknowledged eminence—a German on the one side and an Anglo-Saxon on the other—and in essence their statements are identical. Baron von Stengel, who was Germany's delegate to the first Hague Conference, declares that "every great Power must employ its efforts towards exercising the largest influence possible, not only in European but in world politics, and this mainly because economic power depends in the last resort on political power, and because the largest participation possible in the trade of the world is a vital question for every nation."

On the other side of the world, you have the great Anglo-Saxon writer, Admiral Mahan, urging an exactly similar point of view. Admiral Mahan says:

"The old predatory instinct that he should take who has the power survives . . . and moral force is not sufficient to determine issues unless supported by physical. Governments are corporations, and corporations have no souls; governments, moreover, are trustees, and as such must put first the lawful interests of their wards—their own people. . . . More and more Germany needs the assured importation of raw materials, and, where possible, control of regions productive of such materials. More and more she requires assured markets and security as to the importation of food, since less and less comparatively is produced within her own borders by her rapidly increasing population. This all means security at sea. . . . Yet the supremacy of Great Britain in European seas means a perpetually latent control of German commerce. . . . The world has long been accustomed to the idea of a predominant naval power, coupling it with the name of Great Britain, and it has been noted that such power, when achieved, is commonly often associated with commercial and industrial predominance the struggle for which is now in progress between Great Britain and Germany. Such predominance forces a nation to seek markets, and, where possible, to control them to its own advantage by preponderant force, the ultimate expression of which is possession. . . . From this flow two results: the attempt to possess and the organisation of force by which to maintain possession already achieved. . . . This statement is simply a specific formulation of the general necessity stated; it is an inevitable link in the chain of logical sequences—industry markets, control, navy bases. . . ."*

Thus we get the essence of the whole philosophy which has its final expression in an Armament Bill for Great Britain of over three hundred and fifty million dollars a year, and for the world of something like two billion five hundred million dollars a year, and a situation of such tension that at times it hangs like a nightmare over civilization.

Well, I want to show you that it is the function

* "The Interest of America in International Conditions." Sampson Low, Marston and Co., London.

of banking to play a dominant part in the absolute break-up of this whole philosophy; that this conception has become, by virtue of the forces at work during the last half-century, and especially during the last twenty or thirty years, obsolete; that a nation's prosperity does not and cannot depend upon its military power; that wealth in the modern world has become intangible so far as conquest or confiscation is concerned; that military power can not latently or actively control markets to its own advantage; that, indeed, the whole assumption that the political entity can be made to coincide with the economic entity, in a world in which the economic frontiers expand and contract in infinite degrees and in infinite directions yearly, almost daily, ignores the most potent factors touching the proposition; that political power has ceased to be a determining factor in the economic sphere; that it is an outrageous absurdity to represent a nation, a large part of whose population would starve to death but for the economic co-operation of other nations, as a separate entity struggling against other distinct entities; that nations are no longer such separate organisms, but interdependent parts of the same organism; that the whole biological analogy has been misapplied; and that banking is the final expression of the forces destined to make clear these propositions—to render military force economically futile.

If it can be shown that these propositions are largely and generally true, I think you will agree with me that the modification in political conceptions which banking is destined to bring about, is not incidental or trivial, but fundamental, basic in character, truly what I have called it, revolutionary, destined to play a large part in indicating a way out of what is perhaps the gravest problem to-day affecting our civilization.

I want first to call your attention to this fact: that all these great authorities to whom I have referred assume that the relationship between States is unchangeable in character, that what it has been it always will be, that Aristotle's or Machiavelli's conception of these things is substantially as true of our day as of theirs. Well, now I will put a case to you.

When a Viking king of old landed on these shores from his own State, and hammered his way into a Saxon stronghold, capturing all the cattle and corn and slaves and women that he could lay his hands upon, and squeezing the population for Danegeld, he sailed back to his own State just so much the richer by what he could load on his ships, and when he got back home his own State had practically suffered nothing by the devastation which he might have created in securing his loot. Now imagine a modern, a German Viking landing on British shores, rifling the great national treasury chest, say the vaults of the Bank of England, destroying our railroads, destroying all the commercial records he could lay his hands on, blowing safe deposit vaults into the air, putting into effect, indeed, Blücher's "What a city to sack!" as ruthlessly as he liked, loading his ships with the thirty or forty millions that he could secure in this way, and sailing back to Germany. Would he, like his predecessor of the eighth, ninth, or tenth century, have found that as an offset to the proceeds of his little expedition there was no damage to German trade or to German prosperity? Take one item only—the plunder of the Bank of England's metallic reserve. Remembering the special position of the Bank of England, the relation of its small reserve to the large international business done, and recalling certain incidents in which the State bank of a foreign country at a time when that country was in a political sense bitterly hostile to us, has in quite recent times come to its help, I think many will agree that I am hardly overstating the case in saying that that act of unimaginable economic vandalism would close the Bank of Germany itself. Even if it did not do that, it would involve loss and cost to German finance and trade greatly exceeding in amount the value of the loot secured. An operation of the kind I have described, quite profitable in the old days from the point of view of the invader, would in our days not merely be profitless, but would involve to the conqueror, a loss infinitely greater in amount than the tangible booty which he could secure.

Can we say, therefore, that the international relationship of these two cases is identical, unchanged in character? That plunder, and the motive leading to it, is quite as simple a matter now as then? Of course we cannot. It has fundamentally changed. The whole character of the relationship is different owing to factors introduced by our credit system.

That is not all. I have spoken of the intangibility of wealth. It is intangible in two ways. You, of course, know that most wealth in its modern form depends upon the security of commercial contract, and that if you upset that by overriding the processes of law by military power—if the Courts will not enforce the mortgage bond—the wealth which these instruments represented disappears, in large part at least. The confidence which gives them value has gone. But modern wealth is intangible in a second sense.

The confiscation of wealth on a large national scale has become impossible owing to the damage which would react on the confiscator by virtue of the economic forces which banking embodies, and by virtue of the fact, again owing to banking, that the immense bulk of wealth now consists, not in chattels which can be carried off—transferred by force from one party to another—but in multifarious activities of the community which must imply freedom not only to produce but to enjoy and to consume.

"The glittering wealth of this golden isle," which some political poetaster tells us is so tempting to invaders, consists for the most part in the fact that the population travel a great deal by train, ride in motor cars with rubber tires, propelled by petrol from Russian wells, and eat meat carried on Argentine rivers and wheat on Canadian railways. If the invader reduced the population of these islands to starvation, the "Was für Plunder" of old Blücher's phrase—this booty which so tempts the invader, would have simply vanished into thin air and with it, be it noted—a most important fact—a good deal of the invader's as well.

If this is not intangibility the word has no meaning. Speaking broadly and generally, the conqueror in our day has before him two alternatives: to leave things alone, and in order to do that he need not have left his shores: or to interfere by confiscation in some form, in which case he dries up the source of the profit which tempted him. Just how far this intangibility renders nugatory such devices of conquest as an indemnity, tribute, exclusive markets, when it comes to a question of one great complex industrial community attempting to profit by the parasitic exploitation of another, it is not my present purpose to show. But it is evident we have here, on the very first analysis, two fundamentally important features in which the early pre-economic statecraft would quickly prove unworkable in our day; in which the motives dictating the relationship of States are subject to great modification. It is merely silly to argue (and yet I have heard it argued by a great university professor) that there is no change. All that remains in doubt is the degree of change and its direction: whether it has moved sufficiently far as yet to reach a condition which makes military power economically futile as I have declared.

It is important that we should realise just *how* that relationship has changed: what has been the underlying process at work: what has been the character of the development.

If I appear to wander for a moment from my subject, I would ask you to remember that it is impossible to explain or to have any clear idea of the real significance of any one great fact in the world, without paying at least some attention to the apparently unrelated facts that have produced it.

You remember the nursery story of the plum-pudding that took 200 men to make, and yet, when finally produced, was just an ordinary plum-pudding. And if you cannot explain one plum-pudding save by going back to the ploughman who ploughed the ground, and the sower who sowed the seed for the wheat, and the ship which brought the plums to England, you cannot tell the story of so complex a subject as banking and the relations of States, without going back to the facts which at the first blush do not appear to bear very directly on it. But I shall not digress for more than a minute or two.

Now, the basic fact in the development from the Viking to our own day is the division of labour, little as that may appear on the surface. If there were no division of labour, organized society would never have grown up, because there would have been no necessity for men's co-operation: a man able to do everything necessary for his life himself would be a really independent person, not caring a rap as to whether his neighbours died or lived. Now an exactly similar development is shown in the growth of communities, which are at first independent of others, and then by the division of labour come to be dependent upon them. If in the times of the Danish invasions, England could by some magic have killed all foreigners, she would presumably have been better off. If she could do the same thing to-day half her population would starve to death. The feudal community, which was already a somewhat complex social organization, necessitating all sorts of arts and crafts and sciences, produced in the little domain—the estate of the feudal lord—everything that it needed, and it could be, and was, quite independent of others; it was often cut off by impassable roads for weeks and months at a time from all similar communities, and did not suffer in the least. But if to-day an English county is cut off from other counties by, for instance, a general railroad strike, its whole life is paralyzed in twenty-four hours. This means that the division of labour has rendered it dependent upon others, dependent upon the work of the world going on uninterruptedly.

But the division of labour produces a still further factor, perhaps the most important of all: the subsidence of physical force—the tendency for such to be completely replaced, especially between communities, by the free exchange of goods and services. It is the development from compulsion to freedom, from militarism to commerce, the inevitable drift towards the final elimination of the military factor.

I have illustrated the whole thing elsewhere by a little historical sketch:

When I kill my prisoner (cannibalism was a very common characteristic of early man), it is in "human nature" to keep him for my own larder without sharing him. It is the extreme form of the use of force, the extreme form of human individualism. But putrefaction sets in before I can consume him (it is as well to recall these real difficulties of the early man, because, of course, "human nature does not change"), and I am left without food. But my two neighbours, each with his butchered prisoner, are in like case, and though I could quite easily defend my larder, we deem it better on the next occasion to join forces and kill one prisoner at a time. I share mine with the other two; they share theirs with me. There is no waste through putrefaction. It is the earliest form of the surrender of the use of force in favour of co-operation—the first attenuation of the tendency to act on impulse. But when the three prisoners are consumed, and no more happen to be available, it strikes us that on the whole we should have done better to make them catch game and dig roots for us. The next prisoners that are caught are not killed—a further diminution of impulse and the factor of physical force—they are only enslaved, and the pugnacity which in the first case went to kill them is now diverted to keeping them at work. But the pugnacity is so little controlled by rationalism that the slaves starve, and prove incapable of useful work. They are better treated; there is a diminution of pugnacity. They become sufficiently manageable for the masters themselves, while the slaves are digging roots, to do a little hunting. The pugnacity recently expended on the slaves is redirected to keeping hostile tribes from capturing them—a difficult matter, because the slaves themselves show a disposition to try a change of mastership. They are bribed into good behaviour by better treatment: a further diminution of force, a further drift towards co-operation; they give labour, we give food and protection. As the tribes enlarge, it is found that those have most cohesion where the position of slaves is recognised by definite rights and privileges. Slavery becomes serfdom or villeiny. The lord gives land and protection, the serf labour and military service: a further drift from force, a further drift towards co-operation, exchange. With the introduction of money even the form of force disappears: the labourer pays rent and the lord pays his soldiers. It is free exchange on both sides, and economic force has replaced physical force. The further the drift from force towards simple economic interest the better the result for the effort expended. The Tartar khan, who seizes by force the wealth in his State, giving no adequate return, soon has none to seize. Men will not work to create what they cannot enjoy, so that, finally, the khan has to kill a man by torture in order to obtain a sum which is the thousandth part of what a London tradesman will spend to secure a title carrying no right to the exercise of force from a Sovereign who has lost all right to the use or exercise of physical force, the head of the wealthiest country in the world, the sources of whose wealth are the most removed from any process involving the exercise of physical force.

While this process is going on inside the tribe, or group, or nation, force and hostility between differing tribes or nations remain; but not undiminished. At first it suffices for the fuzzy head of a rival tribesman to appear above the bushes for primitive man to want to hit it. He is a foreigner: kill him. Later, he only wants to kill him if he is at war with his tribe. There are periods of peace: diminution of hostility. In the first conflicts all of the other tribe are killed—men, women, and children. Force and pugnacity are absolute. But the use of slaves, both as labourers and as concubines, attenuates this; there is a diminution of force. The women of the hostile tribe bear children by the conqueror: there is a diminution of pugnacity. At the next raid into the hostile territory it is found that there is nothing to take, because everything has been killed or carried off. So on later raids the conqueror kills the chiefs only (a further diminution of pugnacity, a further drift from mere impulse), or merely dispossesses them of their lands which he divides among his followers (Norman Conquest type). We have already passed the stage of extermination. The conqueror simply absorbs the conquered—or the conquered absorbs the conqueror, whichever you like. It is no longer the case of one gobbling up the other. Neither is gobbled. In the next stage we do not even dispossess the chiefs—a further sacrifice of physical force—we merely impose tribute. But the conquering nation soon finds itself in the position of the khan in his own State—the more he squeezes the less he gets, until, finally, the cost of getting the money by military means exceeds what is obtained. It was the case of Spain in Spanish America—the more territory she "owned" the poorer she became. The wise conqueror, then, finds that better than the exaction of tribute is an exclusive market—old English colonial type. But in the process of ensuring exclusiveness more is lost than is gained: the colonies are allowed to choose their own system—further drift from the use of force, further drift from hostility and pugnacity. Final result: complete abandonment of physical force, co-operation on basis of mutual profit the only relationship, with reference not merely to colonies which have become in fact foreign States, but also to States foreign in name as well as in fact. We have arrived not at the intensification of the struggle between men, but at a condition of vital dependence upon the prosperity of foreigners. Could England by some magic kill all foreigners, half the British population would starve. This is not a condition making indefinitely for hostility to foreigners; still less is it a condition in which such hostility finds its justification in any real instinct of self-preservation or in any deep-seated biological law. With each new intensification of dependence between the parts of the organism must go that psychological development which has marked every stage of the progress in the past, from the day that we killed our prisoner in order to eat him, and refused to share him with our fellow, to the day that the telegraph and the bank have rendered military force economically futile.

But in the foregoing sketches I have purposely left out of account the operation of one factor which is precisely the one most apt to determine the conduct of one group to another, and without which their history might have gone on without greatly modifying the particular relation we are now discussing. And this other factor which I have not specifically illustrated here, is what I have called Sensibility or Organic Consciousness, a capacity on the part of one section of the organism, nation that is, to measure the extent of its dependence upon the rest, and to measure it immediately. And that is the function of banking.

Why do I say that the factors already indicated by my two illustrations would not, of themselves, greatly modify the relationship of States? For this reason: our conduct is determined, not by the facts of the world which affect us, but only by so much of the facts as we can realise—only when we see the relation of cause and effect in those facts. "It is not," says one thinker, "the facts which matter, but men's opinions about facts," and although what I have described does, in fact, describe a condition of real interdependence, the rivalry of States and the growth of armaments might but for this further factor, with which I am going to deal, go on unchecked, as some of my critics declare it will. Those critics point out that there was a certain measure of interdependence between States in the ancient world, that Rome had an elaborate banking system, credit was already an important fact in the world during the Napoleonic struggle, a still more important one when Germany devastated France, trying to cripple her economically as part of a State policy. But I do not think they have taken into consideration the development of sensibility.

Let me illustrate by actual historical cases.

You know the sort of policy which Spain pursued in South America during three centuries: the continent was ruthlessly bled, mainly for its gold. Not merely was the bulk of the output of the mines taken by the Spanish Government, but the whole trade of those vast territories was controlled by

Spain for the benefit ot certain privileged interests in the Mother Country. All goods had to be taken to certain centres and there shipped in a certain way, this sometimes involving mule transportation thousands of miles out of the direct route; and this was merely a detail. Now, the point is this. That policy was not in the long-run profitable to Spain. The country which was having poured into it the gold of half a universe possessed a population which was one of the poorest in Europe at the time. Yet Spanish statesmen went on trying to apply the policy which was ruining them, trying to live on extorted bullion, and for this reason: the relation between the policy that they were applying and its results was too remote to be apparent; the reaction of cause and effect too slow to be observed. Spain, say, passed a law which, for the purpose of some immediate and special gain, spelt absolute ruin to a vast province; but the effect of that ruin did not make itself felt on Spain for perhaps a generation, and there were no means of tracing and registering the effects over so long a period, a period during which other factors would intervene still further to obscure cause and effect, especially at a time when the printed book was practically unknown. It was, therefore, the immediate, the *a priori*, which dominated the statesman's course. He saw that if he had gold in his pockets he could buy what he wanted; therefore he said, "Let's get plenty of gold and keep it from leaving the country, and we shall be all right." The policy which was followed during those three centuries was the mere extortion of bullion, the mercantile theory in all its crudity, with the results that we know. The more that it was enforced the poorer Spain became, and the real condition of interdependence, the real policy which should dominate one country in its relations to another, was quite unrealized.

Now, imagine a modern Spain responsible for the policy of a modern South America, developed industrially and financially to a high degree. We should best understand the relationship, perhaps, if we could imagine the American Revolution not having taken place, and England still "owning," in the meaningless phrase of our politics, North America, and then imagine England to-day trying to introduce the sort of policy which Spain enforced during three hundred years in South America; enacting in Parliament, for instance, that every mine and oil-well in the United States should pay a tribute of 80 per cent. to certain monopolists in London; ordaining that all cotton coming from Louisiana and destined for Lancashire should first be taken to Winnipeg, and there pay a special octroi tax, and then be handled by certain privileged firms, shipped in certain privileged ships at certain fixed rates, and arriving, shall we say, at Deal, because that happened to be the seat of another monopolist, be brought inland, shall we say, to the town of Derby, because that happened to be the seat of a business having influence with the Government, and from Derby shipped to Manchester. You know, of course, that an Act of Parliament of that kind, merely a paraphrase of the sort of legislation enforced by Spain on South America during three hundred years, passed to-day would precipitate a financial crisis, first in America, but immediately after in England, which would involve tens of thousands of business men in London, having, at first sight, but the remotest connection with the interests involved, and would practically annihilate a great national business in Lancashire—on which thousands of our countrymen depend for food. No man would know whether he would find his bank closed in the morning or not.

And this is the point: the result of such an Act would not be felt, as in the case of seventeenth-century Spain, in twenty, thirty, or fifty years, but would be felt within twenty minutes of the time that its provisions became known. Think for a moment of the investments that would be rendered valueless, of the panic with which they would be thrown on to the market, of the chaos that would instantaneously result, and you know that if the business men in Lancashire or London possessed any influence whatsoever with the British Government, all their influence as a matter of life and death would be thrown instantly against that Government, so as to ensure the rescinding of such an impossible law. And this instantaneous effect would be due to processes which banking has devised, availing itself of the telegraph, which enables it, or, rather, compels it, to act by anticipation—before, perhaps, such legislation had actually been enforced at all.

Now, that is what I mean by sensibility or organic consciousness. The Stock Exchange and the bank rate would enable the organism to realise instantly what cruder and less developed organisms could not realise at all, for the simple reason that they possessed no nervous system. Banking provides the organism with its sensory nerves, which means, surely, the capacity to co-ordinate its acts and perform them with a realisation of their effect. And those sensory nerves are the creation of our own time.

That is why I think that a whole body of criticism directed at my work is hardly valid. I am told that the interdependence of nations is an old story; that these factors existed in the past, and that they did not deprive military force of its advantage, or, if they did, that fact did not modify the conduct of one state to another. But the determining factor, which is the immediate reaction I have attempted to indicate, the only thing which will really affect policy, did not and could not exist. The intellectual conception of these truths may be old, but their demonstration, in such a way as to affect the general public opinion which dictates the policy of nations, is new. And the historical demonstration of this is very simple.

The interdependence of nations was first argued

seriously in the modern world by Hume in 1752. He was followed by Adam Smith in a work of far wider reach, thirty years later. Yet their arguments had evidently not affected general policy at the end of the eighteenth century, as political discussion in England at the time of the American Revolution, and on the Continent at the time of the Napoleonic wars, showed plainly enough. Indeed, the practical, vital interdependence of States was then very small, as the results of Napoleon's Continental system clearly showed. Even England, industrially the most developed of all, was only dependent upon foreigners (except occasionally in years of great scarcity) for luxuries, spices, wines, brandies, silks—things which, while the trade in them was considerable, affected only an infinitesimal part of the population, and which were not much affected by the prosperity or otherwise of the neighbouring peoples. England had not yet a great national industry which depended upon the prosperity of her neighbours—upon, that is, the neighbours being able to send her food and raw material in abundant quantities, upon their being able to carry on their industries. This is the crucial test of vital interdependence, and it did not exist in any country in the world at the beginning of the nineteenth century. England was nearer to it by half a century than any other country. Indeed, we might even say that as late as the last quarter of the nineteenth century there was not a single nation in the world outside Britain illustrating, in the daily needs of vast masses of its population, this sort of vital dependence upon its neighbours, in the way, for instance, that Lancashire is dependent upon American cotton, or in the way upon which millions of our people are upon foreign food. Consequently, until well into the nineteenth century, despite the intellectual labours of the physiocrats, the old idea that it was to a nation's interest to kill the industry of other nations was still predominant. But by the third or fourth decade of the nineteenth century a real division of labour had set in. Steam was now playing a large rôle in our industry, and when our cheap coal placed us in an advantageous condition to make ready use of that force, and our geographical position (corresponding in a world, which included America, precisely to the position which the Venetian Republics held when the world was mainly the Mediterranean) assisted the development of our industries, foreign trade began to render cheap food essential to our population. A few bad harvests, "the rain that rained away the Corn Laws," showed our dependence upon foreign food. And that dependence created a revolution in fiscal policy. A change of ideas which all the splendid arguments of the physiocrats had been unable to effect in a hundred years, was brought about by the absolute demonstration of our need for foreign food in five.

And this change synchronized roughly with a change in our whole conception of the relationship of one country to another—a frank abandonment of the old relationship of exploitation by the Mother Country towards the Colonies; the complete acceptance of the idea of self-government for our overseas possessions. A moment's reflection, indeed, convinces one that this conception of the relationship of the mother community to great daughter communities is the direct logical outcome of that change in the idea of the relationship of nations which the physiocrats had taught, and which events had made understandable.

But a nation is not a person. It is only our careless speech which leads us to say that "England" is in favour of that, or "Germany" of this; forty millions or sixty millions are never all of the same mind. And although the defeat of the old political notion seemed pretty complete when Cobden had done his work, there were very many in the country who still firmly believed that what England had most to fear was the growth of power and prosperity in other nations. This received a curious illustration at the outbreak of the North and South War in America. The growth of the American Union had disturbed the dreams of many English statesmen, and when, at the outbreak of war, it appeared that that Union was about to break up, very little trouble was taken on the part of many Englishmen to hide their satisfaction at the prospect. The very first result of that impending break-up of a foreign State, however, was the partial ruin of a great industry, and the starvation of tens of thousands of work-people, in our own State. The essential interdependence of peoples received a further economic illustration, which was another nail in the coffin of the old ideas. Note the development in political ideas. In 1860 it was still part of British policy—still part of the ideas of the men who governed England—to prevent the development of the United States. How much of such a policy is left to-day? Who believes that a wealthy United States is a danger to this country?

Let us get back to the Continent, however, with this historical sketch. While England's prosperity had yet for a generation been bound up vitally with the work of other nations—getting her grain and meat from America, her wool from Australia—the Continental nations, without an exception, were still, despite the fact that several possessed large trades, built up on the export of luxuries like wine and silks, roughly self-sufficing and self-supporting; and their policy showed it.

In 1870 Louis Napoleon saw with dismay the possibility of a German Union, and it had on him pretty much the same effect in 1870 as the spectre of a great American Union had had on English statesmen in 1860; and acting on the old idea that the power of a neighbour must necessarily be used against you and his prosperity be inimical to your own (in one sense he was right, because that was precisely the motive animating all nations, except England, which was just beginning to learn the real lesson), he directed his policy towards crushing that power and crippling that prosperity —that is to say, he encouraged a line of policy which tended to render the consolidation of the German States difficult and incomplete. Bismarck challenged the interference successfully, and used his force by deliberately trying to crush France, not merely in a political, but in an economic sense. It was his avowed intention so to adjust things that never again should France be an economic Power in Europe. There was no economic relationship between the two peoples to pull him up smartly in the matter; no German Lancashire to starve because French cotton-fields were overrun with soldiers. German industry did not depend either upon French wheat or French money. Well, note what follows. Germany settled down to consolidate her political and economic position, gave herself over to intense industry and commercial development, which followed pretty much the same lines that similar development in England had followed in the preceding generation. And after forty years of this economic development came another Franco-German conflict; once more the armies were ranged face to face, and a German statesman, frankly basing his policy on the Bismarckian philosophy, stood once more in Bismarck's place, with these great advantages, however, over his predecessor: where Bismarck had represented a Germany of forty millions confronting a France of the same number, a Germany, moreover, which was not yet politically united, Herr von Kiderlen Waechter represented a Germany of sixty-five millions as against a France of thirty-eight millions, a Germany which had had forty years of political union and severe discipline, and a Germany which had grown enormously, inconceivably, while France had stood still. But there was no war. Where Bismarck could have bled France white with a certain satisfaction, without any immediate damage being involved to his own country, Herr von Kiderlen Waechter (I am told to his surprise) learned that to bleed white this relatively feeble France of 1911 would be to plunge this great and powerful Germany into the direst economic distress. What American cotton had been to Lancashire in 1865, French money, and all that it directly and indirectly represents, was to German industry in 1911. He learned, still more to his surprise apparently, that of the twenty million souls added to German population since 1870, nearly all were dependent upon foreign food, and gained their livelihood from industries dependent to a large extent upon foreign capital, most of it French and English capital, and that, if by some magic the ultimate Bismarckian dream of wiping France economically from the map of Europe could be realised, he would be prevented, and, indeed, was prevented, from carrying it out, not by any consideration for French welfare, but by the very pressing necessities of German industry, and by the direct influence of German financiers and German business men. The very threat of it was enough. Did it leak out that German demands had become unacceptable, there was a slump on the Berlin Bourse, and some German industrial bank closed its doors; did the German jingoes talk of the imminence of war, the bank rate moved up a point, and some considerable German house went into insolvency. I could trace for you, if I had the time, a really humorous chart establishing the direct relationship between the "vigour" of German foreign policy and the figures ot German commercial insolvency.

The condition is indeed well described by our own Consul-General in Germany—Sir Francis Oppenheimer—who points out in his last report that the close alliance between the banks and the industries in Germany creates a situation which—I use his very words—"must in times of international crisis result in general collapse." From numberless similar comments I take the following from the Bourse *Gazette* of Berlin:

> "The policy which the Government has been pursuing since July 1 has inflicted on our commerce and our industry losses almost as great as they would have suffered from an unsuccessful war."

Such an opinion may be exaggerated; that is not the point. The point is that financial opinion is already feeling this effect of policy. What I am saying is this: These nerves about which I have talked were already acting on the organism, already beginning to affect public opinion, which in its turn would be bound, sooner or later, to affect the Government. And, indeed, we have complete evidence that such opinion, stirred by these financial nerves, did very rapidly influence the policy of the Government. Here is an incident typical of many similar things which were going on at the time, told in a *Times* telegram from Berlin.

We were in the midst of a pessimistic period, and the German Government had with evident intent been assiduously issuing pessimistic notes. The *Times* telegram was as follows:

"One consequence of the disquieting semi-official statements was that a considerable time before the opening of the Bourse numerous selling orders began to arrive, and there seemed every prospect of another heavy fall in prices. The principal banking institutions, however, put themselves immediately in communication with the Foreign Office, and at an early hour several of the representatives of the great banks, including, it is stated, Herr von Helfferich, Director of the Deutsche Bank, Herr Carl Furstenburg, Director of the Berlin Handelsgesellschaft, and the representatives of the National Bank and the house of Bleichroeder, were received at the Foreign Office by Herr Zimmerman, the Under-Secretary of State for Foreign Affairs, who, in reply to inquiries, made reassuring statements of the most positive kind with regard to the situation. Encouraged by these assurances, the banks lent their support, with the result that prices were maintained at a satisfactory level throughout the day."

Could we have clearer evidence that Germany had arrived at a time when its Government was modifying its policy of aggression in response to those new economic needs that had come to make Germany dependent upon the financial security of its neighbours?

How far are we removed from the glorious days when Bismarck could glibly talk of bleeding France white with the satisfactory assurance that not a German would be the poorer in consequence, and that, on the contrary, the German State would immensely gain thereby? This illustrates the social Law of Acceleration which I have attempted to explain elsewhere: Bismarck was nearer to being able to apply the methods of Attila, some fifteen hundred years removed from him, than we are to being able to apply the methods of Bismarck, from whom only forty years separate us.

I know what you will say: That it was not these considerations which prevented war, but the fact that Germany, in addition to the French Army, had also to face the British Navy. But I beg you to remember that there have been two Morocco incidents in the last ten years, and on the first occasion the English Navy did *not* stand in any special sense behind France; and if you will examine the German financial press of that period, you will find that precisely the same order of economic and commercial considerations which played so great a weight in dictating the lines of general policy in 1911 played also a predominant, though not so noticeable a rôle in dictating German policy in 1905. "There can be no doubt," says one credible French authority, "that war was prevented by reason of Germany's industrial dependence upon international credit." And the same authority adds this significant note: "The influence of this international economic solidarity is increasing, despite ourselves. It has not resulted from conscious action on the part of any of us, and it certainly cannot be arrested by any conscious action on our part."

I do not say that the political and military factors, the British Navy and the rest of it, did not count. Fifty equally well-informed persons will give fifty divergent opinions as to the respective weight of the factors which have determined this or that action in the case of a Government. A man who has lived all his life at the very centre of things in Germany, and who is in touch, not only with the commercial, financial, and journalistic worlds, but with the Court and with political subjects, has told me this:

"I have watched many political developments and intrigues, and have shared in many; perhaps I have seen as much of the inside of German policy as any man, and you ask me whether the future holds war or peace, and I have to tell you that I do not know. You ask me whether Germany is in favour of peace, and again I have to say I do not know. The Emperor does not know whether Germany favours war or peace, though he personally most certainly would favour peace; but he cannot tell whether his efforts will prevail."

And yet you get people who talk of a country—say Germany—as though its acts were the outcome of a fixed opinion, like that formed by an individual having definitely made up its mind to do this or to do that, not the expression of a body of opinion, subject to modification by all sorts of forces, a thing perpetually in a state of flux. There is not a Government in Europe that has not radically changed its views on policy in ten years. In 1900 France was in deadly opposition to England. English opinion would hear nothing good of France and nothing bad of Germany. Fifteen years since Anglophobia was one of the dominating factors in American foreign policy. And you may take the wildest expression of Anglophobia to be found in Germany to-day, and I will duplicate it by a similar outburst from some prominent American of that period. Again, we are told that the German Government does not care a rap about what the financial world and the banks may think, and how they may suffer from its policy. Well, I will say nothing of the fact that all the evidence goes against this, and that the history I have just recounted is a direct denial of it. But surely we must realize that in the end the Government *is* the world of affairs, in the sense that the general trend of its policy must sooner or later be determined by the interests and the necessities of the mass of the people from which it derives its power, its money, its general capacity to act with efficiency and precision. A modern war, of all things, involves that capacity which a Government must derive from acting in the long-run in connection with the great currents, economic and moral, of its time and people. It is not possible for any great State taking an active part in the life of the world to do otherwise. The State simply is powerless before these currents.* Not only has the work of the German people unintentionally brought to nought the carefully laid plans of the statesman, but modern Germany would have been impossible unless those plans *had* miscarried. It was Bismarck's declared policy from first to last to check, by every possible means, the economic development of France. She was to be blotted out as an

*This address was delivered in January, 1912, and on July 11, 1913, the British Chancellor of the Exchequer (Mr. Lloyd George) speaking at the Mansion House said: "Two years ago the financial interests of the Continent, I believe, stopped a war. And I believe that it is only these great financial interests that will be able effectually to intervene in order to arrest this terrible growth (of armaments). . . . There is one advantage they have got Finance is international the present condition of things proves it. If there is trouble in one country the finance of the next is affected. There is war in the East and the West bleeds. Banks fall in the West and the East trembles."

economic factor in Europe. Well, if she had been, the wonderful development of German commerce in the last twenty years would have been impossible.

That commerce is largely with such countries as South America, the Near East, Russia; and the recent development of those countries, which makes the large German trade possible, is due mainly to French and English capital. If German statesmen had really been able to wipe out Germany's rivals, this development of German trade would not have taken place.

And all the efforts of French statesmen to control these currents have, on their side, been just as futile. French policy has aimed at fortifying Russia to counterbalance Germany, and, with that purpose, an alliance with Russia was formed, an integral part of the understanding being that a portion of the immense free capital of France should be available for Russia. The capital was given, with the result that German trade in Russia, thanks to development due in no small measure to this French capital, has gone up from about 15 to 45 per cent., and Germany may be said to-day commercially to dominate Russia. It is one of the great outlets for German industrial and commercial activity—thanks to the very policy which was aimed against Germany.

And note this: that with the freedom of communication in every sense that now exists in the world, it has become a material impossibility to prevent French money from aiding German trade in one form or another. So long as France, with a stationary population and large amounts of free capital, desires interest on her money; so long as the French father desires to give his daughter a dot; so long, in other words, as France achieves in some measure those aims for which mainly the State exists at all, her money will go to the help of German trade.

And note also how the division of labour which sets up, as I have explained, the mutual dependence of nations the one upon the other is not merely intensified, but actually created, by the force of credit. We know that a difference of a few pence per ton in the cost of coal, and a few shillings in the cost of wheat, is sufficient to make one country mainly a coal-producing country, and another mainly a wheat-producing country, and that the establishment of that difference of a few pence or a few shillings would not have been possible except for the services which modern credit is able to render to the world of commerce; but there is a form of division of labour—and a form which is most important in the circumstances we are considering—directly due to the devices of banking. Before 1870 France had as large a population as she has to-day, and she was, relatively to other countries in Europe, already a wealthy and saving one. Yet the amount of foreign investments made every year under the Empire was not one-tenth of the amount which is made to-day by a smaller population.* It is a demonstration of how the financial factor in the affairs of the world is growing, not proportionately to population, but absolutely. Multitudinous factors since the war—of which the extermination by war of the bold and adventurous type of man is certainly one—have contributed to make France a nation of very small families, cautiously saving for the future, endowing their one son or their one daughter with capital or a dot, so that an immense amount of money is liberated for investment abroad; whereas in the case of Germany a new population of twenty millions have had to be started in the world, and the capital thus called for has more than absorbed all that Germany could save. But it is the devices of banking which enable the two countries to divide their labour according to their characteristics, one being a maker of capital, and the other a user of capital. And because you have created this division of labour by virtue of the work of banking, you have also created that condition of dependence of the one upon the other which I have tried to indicate at the beginning of this address. The very stagnation of France which set free this capital is precisely the factor which makes it impossible for Germany to crush her.

Now, I want you to recall for a moment the

* See the very striking figures given in this connection in "Le Rôle des Établissements de Crédit en France" (published by *La Revue Politique et Parliamentaire*, Paris).

propositions with which I started this paper, namely, that the relations of States are rapidly modifying in obedience to changing conditions—the greater division of labour set up by quicker communications; that this intensified division of labour sets up a condition of necessary interdependence between those who share the labour; that this condition of interdependence in its turn involves a necessary subsidence of the factor of physical force between them; that this subsidence of physical force not only weakens necessarily the rôle of political control, but the very complexity of the division of labour tends to set up co-operation in groups which cut right athwart political frontiers, so that the political no longer limits or coincides with the economic frontier; and that, finally, partly as the cumulative effect of all these factors, and partly as the direct effect of devices born of the necessity of co-ordinating such factors, you get what I may term telegraphic financial reaction—a condition of sensibility by which the organism as a whole becomes quickly conscious of any damage to a part; that the matter may be summarised in the statement that military force is more and more failing in its effect, and must finally become—I think it has already become—economically futile. Just remember those propositions, and then recall the facts of the historical sketch which I have just given you, and ask yourself whether they are not confirmed in every single detail.

At the beginning of that story we find a marauding State inflicting all the damage that physical force can inflict and suffering itself little harm. At the end of the story we get a condition in which a State cannot inflict damage anything like as great without such damage reacting disastrously on the State inflicting it. At the beginning we have an England which could have seen all its political rivals annihilated without damage; at the end we have an England in which such a thing would spell starvation to its population. At the beginning, a Power like Spain, able to exercise military force as fantastically as it pleased, to bleed to its apparent profit another people; at the end a condition in which the use of military force in any such way would be fatal to the prosperity of the country so using it. At the beginning, interdependence so slow of growth that two thousand years hardly shows a development therein; at the end the interdependence growing so rapidly and becoming so sensitive that, having no effect on the policy of a great Continental State in the third quarter of the nineteenth century, it dominates that policy in the first decade of the twentieth. However you may test the general propositions I have laid down by the history of human development, you will find that they stand that test absolutely.

They stand this test because the condition which I have attempted to indicate is not merely a condition of the relationship of one nation to another, it is the essential condition of the relationship of all men to all other men individually. The forces which I have been trying to illustrate are the forces which have made possible organised society.

And just one word as to the immediate practical outcome.

Need I say that I do not expect universal peace to dawn a week next Tuesday morning, nor do I believe that we should turn our "Dreadnoughts" into colliers, disband our army, and invite the foreigners to come and walk over us. But I do believe that a more thorough examination of the principles I have hinted at here will affect the attitude of the foreigner to us and ours to him, and that in the direction of these principles will be found finally a way out of the absurd *impasse* into which sheer military rivalry, tempered in no way by rationalism, has landed us; that the more thorough discussion of the facts which I have pointed to here is bound to lead to a modification of that public opinion which sets up this rivalry from which we all suffer so much. And our progress towards that will be measured above all by the rapidity with which our intelligence seizes the facts of the change here operating. It cannot be too often repeated that the determining factor in progress is more and more this conscious adaptation of the organism to its environment, which means, in the case of society, human intelligence and the extent to which that force guides instead of allowing itself to be overruled by prejudice, temper, and blind passion.

There are those of course who will tell you that the whole thing is very regrettable; that it is sordid that the conduct of men or nations should be guided by what they are pleased to call money considerations. Well, it all depends on what you mean by money. You of course realise that banking and credit are not things that can exist apart from commerce as a whole. Credit devices (to return to an earlier illustration) are the sensory nerves of the economic organisation, and nerves cannot exist independently from the organism of which they are a part; they cannot live suspended in air. They are important because their condition—of pain or satisfaction—indicates an ill or well working body as the case may be. Banking operations are the co-ordinated expression of all industrial and commercial operations and cannot exist apart from them. Your bill of exchange is not merely a piece of paper; it represents ultimately a cargo of wheat, and the cargo of wheat is not merely merchandise but bread, and bread is not merely dead matter, because it is human food, it connotes human energy and life, "the marvellous chemistry by which a loaf of bread is changed into the melody of Liszt" or the laughter of a child.

Whilst the statesman, the diplomat, the dilettante of high politics, imagining to themselves some dream world where nations are wild warring things living upon one another, to be thrown at one another in some grand series of Armageddons, go on repeating the aphorisms of Aristotle, Charlemagne, or Machiavelli, the silent forces of the great business which this Institute embodies have been defeating their best-laid plans, reducing their machinations to nought, producing the very opposite result to that attempted. Where *they* thought to destroy *you* have built up, where they thought to build up you have destroyed, where they thought to push nations apart you have bound them together with links of steel.

Genuine banking must be built up on a basis of the prosperity of the community as a whole. The condition by which one group can make huge profits by the disasters of another, unhealthy speculation, booms, swindles, are deadly enemies of the sort of banking which this Institute represents. It stands, and must stand, in close alliance with sound trading, the prosperity of the people as a whole. I was discussing this matter once with a great French banker and his friends, and one of them said to me: "I hope you are wrong because if not it seems to me that the banker will be our master. It is the golden age of the Money Power with a vengeance." My friend took this critic by the sleeve and led him to the window, Outside was a queue of people waiting to subscribe to a city loan which had just then been floated in Paris. "You see that line of people?" the banker said. "Well, if that line is not there, the Money Power *has* no power. The money with which we carry on our operations and make our profits and wield our 'power' as you call it, is the money of the public, and the first condition of our prosperity is that the public must have money, that they shall carry on their trade actively and busily, create and consume, buy and sell, both well and wisely. Our prosperity at least is based on the general well-being, which is not the case with some callings that have perhaps greater honour."

But what does general prosperity imply? It implies all those efforts by which the men, women, and children of the world are fed and clothed and housed and warmed, educated in youth, cared for in old age and sickness. If instead of misusing a word to which ancient and irrational prejudice attaches, one uses a little imagination and sees what money and banking really represent, how different an aspect does the whole thing assume!

I have had to meet an immense deal of bitter criticism based on the idea that I am hailing the stockbroker and the banks as the saviours of society; that this is a money-lender's gospel. One critic tells me that my doctrines are "grossly offensive to men of European tradition"—the appeal to human avarice against the profession of arms.

I wanted to know which European tradition. There was a very old and very obstinate European tradition that men who differed from you in ideas—especially in ideas that mattered—should not be listened to and considered but destroyed, burned, tortured, and imprisoned. Perhaps it has been one of the most pregnant traditions—pregnant of evil that is—that has ever dominated the European mind, and coloured European public policy. With it quite naturally and logically went a hostility to the recognition of the laws of natural phenomena which, had not the tradition in question been broken, would have rendered impossible most of that development of human society which I have indicated in this paper; the division of labour, which implies the organisation and systematization of men's tasks—science in its widest sense—would not have taken place, and the human solidarity, the breaking-down of political, racial, and religious barriers, with the intenser co-operation which the whole thing demands, would not have grown up. The larger comradeship which that co-operation implies would have been impossible.

But perhaps of all the evils which pernicious traditions have bequeathed—the prohibition of interest which would have made commerce impossible, that ban upon research and science which would have made invention impossible, that attempt to control ideas by law and force which would have made human society impossible—of all these evils perhaps one of the most vicious is this: that we have been taught to believe there is some necessary contradiction between interest and morality, that high ideals must be in conflict with material advantage, that the higher welfare of the race is in some wonderful way founded upon a sacrifice of its material welfare, that the activities by which the world lives, those by which society has been organised, are not those with which the highest ideals of man can be in any way concerned, those round which the larger common policy of men should be grouped.

I have read somewhere, I think it was in one of Mr. Hartley Withers's books, of a notable discussion which took place among American bankers as to all the factors which made London the financial centre of the universe, and one of them made this profound remark, or in words to this effect: "We may talk of bank reserves, of currency reforms, of anything you will, but one of the most important facts which makes London the centre of the world of banking is the psychological reserve with which the bankers work." You know what he meant by "psychological reserve," he meant the wisdom, the probity, and at times the courage with which the English bankers protect the interests that are confided to them. Unless you have that, the whole edifice is unsound. It is a factor so essential that without it, the whole thing would collapse like a house of cards. It is something which no temptation of high profits or speculative gains can shake. You know of course that the history of banking in the past is full of instances where the refusal of bankers to be bullied by Governments, cajoled by rulers and statesmen, frightened by rivals, tempted by high profits, has time and again saved the solvency of thousands and protected the well-being and happiness of millions.

You I know would be the last to want me to indulge in highfaluting in this matter, but you cannot disassociate the moral from the material side in this matter. That confidence, a real sense of mutual obligation, and the knowledge that those obligations will be unfalteringly fulfilled is, of course, the very essence of successful banking, the very foundation upon which the well-being of any commercial community must be founded, all the cynical critics of commercialism notwithstanding. Indeed we can show by the facts of credit what can be shown in no other way of which I am aware: our present urgent need to do our duty and to keep our faith not merely to communities on the other side of the world that we have never seen but to the communities of posterity, the communities that are not yet born. The solvency of some of our greatest commercial institutions, the fortunes of men actually present in the room, are dependent upon our doing the utmost to see that obligations which will not have to be executed for perhaps half a century and in favour of persons not yet born are made possible of fulfilment. I refer, of course, to the great industry of insurance though the same thing is true in lesser degree of a whole range of industries and financial operations.

There is something uncanny in the thought that the devices of credit enable us thus to be held not merely through our old loans by the dead hand of the past but to be held just as firmly by the hands of generations yet unborn and compel us, willy-nilly, to do our duty to the unknown future. I mention this merely to point out how indissolubly the whole work of civilization is bound up with the fact of credit; to indicate the nature of the cement which it has introduced into our social future; how impossible it is because of it for us to escape our obligations; how its infinite ramifications must more and more compel to good social conduct.

I do not urge, as it has been suggested, that bankers are the "saviours of society." I would, of course, on this occasion like to pay you all the compliments I can, but you are only the saviours of society in the sense in which all those who perform well any vital social function are the saviours of society—essential to it. But your profession has done and is doing much in a special sense, to destroy the ancient and evil illusion I have just touched on.

This condition of commercial interdependence, which is the special mark of banking as it is the mark of no other profession or trade in quite the same degree—the fact that the interest and the solvency of one is bound up with the interest and solvency of many; that there must be confidence in the due fulfilment of mutual obligation, or whole sections of the edifice crumble, is surely doing a great deal to demonstrate that morality after all is not founded upon self-sacrifice, but upon enlightened self-interest, a clearer and more complete understanding of all the ties which bind us the one to the other. And such clearer understanding is bound to improve, not merely the relationship of one group to another, but the relationship of all men to all other men, to create a consciousness which will make for more efficient human co-operation, a better human society.

NOTE

That the recognition of the facts sketched in the foregoing address is beginning to appeal to alert and open minds in diplomacy and practical affairs may be gathered from the more recent works in statecraft and diplomacy. I have had occasion several times in this book to show by citation that most accepted authorities in diplomacy were until lately strongly under the influence of the Machiavellian tradition. Yet how far a man like Dr. David Jayne Hill, who was the American Ambassador to the German Court and who is the author of "A History of Diplomacy in the International Development of Europe" (Oxford University Press), has progressed beyond what he himself calls that "Classic Diplomacy which is based on the assumption that every state is seeking to appropriate for itself everything in the world that possesses value and is restrained from actually doing so only by the resistance it may encounter," is shown by the following passage taken from his later work "World Organization and the Modern State."

"International spoliation has ceased to be a trade. Yet all the old traditions of depredations from beyond the border, of peaceful commerce exposed to capture at sea, of crushing indemnities to be paid by the vanquished to the invading conqueror are kept alive, and serve to thrill the readers of sensational publications, and to force the assent of Parliamentary Committees to extravagant military appropriations. 'Fear and distrust,' the 'natural enemy' just across the frontier, the secret treaties expected to exist between our neighbours—all these linger on,—creating the mirage of terror and suspicion that fills the sky only because there is a background of mist on which alarming images are painted by a sun that has set!

"'But no,' it will be said, 'the light of yesterday has not departed. These fears are well grounded. Our natural enemy is stronger than we; and he will, therefore, avenge himself upon us.' Acting upon this assurance, we strive to become stronger than he; and now this 'natural enemy' says, with all honesty, 'an assault is imminent. We must prepare to resist it.' And so, by a process of endless circular reasoning the illusion of hatred and hostility is kept alive.

"It seems rather remarkable, that Governments, who should be the first to dispell this illusion, are the most belated of all in perceiving that great changes have taken place in the relations of people. Across the frontier there is another civilised people, with a jural consciousness as deep, as enlightened, and as anxious as our own. We loan them, or they loan us, vast sums of money; exchanging hundreds of millions of dollars of securities, on the faith of our railroads, our municipalities, even our governments. Will these debts ever be paid? In the time when our nearest neighbour, stronger than we, was really our 'natural enemy,' and really would have invaded our territory and annexed us, securities and all, it is doubtful if they would have been paid; but no one now doubts that they will be. Bankers do not doubt it, investors do not doubt it; why then should Governments believe, that these same people, who expect to pay their debts, are meditating invasion and conquest, with all that they imply? Simply because they have no serious assurance to the contrary.

"And so it happens, that the modern State, the embodiment of law and the protagonist of justice, whose simple promise to pay is bought by the million in the open market by the shrewdest interpreters of human intentions—the bankers and money lenders—permits itself to be discredited by a dogma of diplomacy which sounds to every honest man like a calumny on human decency.

"It is not necessary to prove that human nature has changed, or will change, or that men are in any degree less self-regarding or inspired by a loftier altruism than prevailed in former times. It is simply that humanity has discovered a new path, and is disposed to follow it. It is perceived that happiness can be obtained more easily and more surely by industry than by plunder, by commerce than by piracy, by intercourse between the nations than by isolation. It is, therefore, necessary to reckon with the new social forces and the new standard of conduct that have come into being through improved transportation, practically instantaneous communication, the discovery of new natural resources, and of new forms of energy to render them available.

"It is important to consider also, that the modern State, affording more equal opportunities, and covering productive effort with the ægis of its protection, has changed the whole nature of society. The individual is probably no less egoistic than before, but the new avenues of profitable activity are open to his enterprise."

WAR AS A CAPITALIST VENTURE

The following article* dealt at greater length with the general idea that it is to the interest of financiers to promote war and deserves, perhaps, reproduction in this connection:

Financiers and War

You know the story of the Coffin Trust in the Chinese Province at a time of plague; how when at the outbreak the Viceroy began to apply sanitary measures he and the whole Provincial Government were presented with shares in the Coffin Trust, with the result that the authorities forthwith encouraged popular prejudice against modern sanitary measures; the plague raged unchecked, and the Coffin Trust paid large dividends. Moral: The Coffin Trust "finance" is at the bottom of plague in China.

For six months Europe has been living on a volcano; the well-being of three hundred millions, more or less, has been in jeopardy, the happiness of generations threatened because a camorra of concession-mongers have been carrying on back-stairs intrigues in order to concoct "deals." Moral: International finance is at the bottom of war in Europe.

Well, I do not believe that either conclusion is the right one; but, on the contrary, that both are due to a

* From the London *Daily Mail* of January 3, 1912.

somewhat muddle-headed confusion, which is particularly mischievous in that it is likely to lead us woefully astray concerning the real nature of the forces at work around us.

What is the quiet, evident, and simple truth in this matter? It is *that a relatively infinitesimal group of financiers is able, by manipulating a mass of ignorance and blind prejudice, to profit at the expense of all other financiers whatsoever.* It would be truer to say of plague that it is a financial interest than to say of war that it is one; those outside the "Trust" may escape plague; very few financiers outside the armament and concession group would escape the damage of war.

What is "international finance"? Is it a small band of Frankfort bankers with foreign names living by the exploitation of people less unscrupulous than themselves? That is a picture lending itself to dramatic and sensational treatment, but it does not happen to be true. All bankers, merchants, investors, those who insure their lives, who have holdings in stocks or shares of any kind, are financiers in the sense that they are interested in the security of wealth and the better organisation of finance. Even when we use the term "financier" in its narrow sense we imply generally a man whose fortune is based upon the general prosperity: if the world as a whole did not make and save and invest money, financiers could not make it—their occupation would be gone. And more and more is it true that modern finance, whether in the large or in the limited sense, is bound up with general security and prosperity; the more that becomes evident the less is the incentive to oppose any special interest to the general one. In a prosperous China, Chinese financiers would not invest in the Coffin Trust, they would find a better way to use money than to speculate in an industry which depended upon the foundations of all wealth being threatened. And the same is true of investments that depend for their success on war.

It is true, of course, that wherever you get conditions in which, on the one hand the general interest is very ill-conceived and the general public very ill-informed, subject to gusts of blind prejudice readily and easily stirred into life, and on the other hand a particular interest well conceived and subject to no such influence, you will get the particular interest controlling the general, five or fifty or five hundred men manipulating as many millions to their own personal advantage. But no mechanical reshaping of society could ever prevent such a result if you get these two elements in juxtaposition. And that is true, not merely in the domains of finance and politics but in things like religion or medicine. It is the story of priestcraft, quackery, demagogism, through all the ages.

There was a time in Europe when massacre and cruelties of all sorts, credulity, and quaking fear of the unseen, passed for religion with great masses of the population. And while that was true, a camarilla of priests could make playthings of nations. The relation which that sort of "religion" bore to morals in Europe in the past the wicked rubbish that too often passes for patriotism bears to politics to-day.

Just think of the history of the last two years. Consider one typical incident. Here is an informed and educated man, the Professor of a great University,*

*The reference is to the interview with Professor Delbrück which appeared in the *Daily Mail* of December 27, 1912, and

telling his countrymen how Great Britain had on three separate occasions plotted to make war on them in cold blood and to attack them without warning. He is, of course, sincere and really believes this thing.

Now if that belief is possible in the case of one of the most educated men on the Continent, one of whose specialities is political history, what may we not expect from the common ruck of the workaday world who have no time to examine things carefully or to weigh evidence?

And this incident, of course, is not peculiar to Germany. It is the exact measure of our wisdom in like matters. I will take the most outrageous manifestation of Anglophobia which you can find in Germany to-day and duplicate it by an exactly similar manifestation from American public men and newspapers of fifteen years ago. I have heard a popular American senator declare that it was America's manifest duty to annihilate Great Britain, that America had to "fight England or float a dead whale on the ocean."

Wherever such a mixture of credulity, ignorance, and sectional prejudice is justified by high-falutin' appeals to patriotism, where respectable public men can directly encourage it by the "my country, right or wrong," nonsense—as though so to act that one's country does wrong instead of right, to direct by our influence and our vote that our nation does the foolish thing instead of the wise, were the way to serve one's country—you will get a condition of things in which the trade and industry of millions will be bled for the personal profit of a few unscrupulous and intriguing

---

which caused much discussion both in England and on the Continent.

men, just as in the domain of religion priestcraft has been known to profit by credulity, passion, and prejudice. But the progress which has been made towards better religious conceptions can be made, and more easily, towards better political conceptions; what the mind of man has done for religion it can certainly do for patriotism.

It cannot be too often repeated that the necessary profitlessness of war between civilized nations, the necessary interdependence of nations, will not stop war. It is the general recognition of profitlessness and interdependence that will stop war. Impersonal forces, the Stock Exchange, and the rest of it, will certainly push these truths more and more into our notice. But the rapidity with which we shall arrive at a better condition of things depends, as every other part of man's struggle for life depends, on the extent to which he brings his intelligence to bear on the matter. The rate of real progress is the rate of improvement in ideas. And when our ideas as to the real relationship of nations have become somewhat saner, it will no longer be possible for intriguing statesmen or concession-hunters to explode these magazines of ignorance and passion. All their intrigues will fizzle out as harmlessly as a wax vesta on a cement floor.

IV

THE PLACE OF MILITARY FORCE IN MODERN STATECRAFT

(An address delivered before the Royal United Service Institution, October 8, 1913, Major-General Sir Thomas Fraser, K.C.B., C.M.G., in the chair.)

It is not specifically the soldier's business to discuss policy, but to execute it if called on to do so. Yet, apart from the fact—more emphasized in the German school of statecraft than our own—that war is inevitably part of policy, and that its conduct, even, is directly affected by the nature of the policy that dictates it, the soldier may be forgiven a little human curiosity as to what the fighting is about, what part his work plays in the general scheme of things in the world.

The astonishing thing is how little attention we have given in England to the relation between war and policy in the largest sense. We have great students of war and we have great students of policy, but our study is generally in water-tight compartments, and the relation between the two is for the most part marked by an extraordinary hiatus, filled in sometimes with a series of apophthegms as, that war represents the policing of mankind, or the struggle for survival, or the expression of a spiritual need for action, mankind's purge of the decadent, and much more to the same effect, concerning which one may say with certainty this: that whatever war may be, it is none of these things.

Any discussion of the general problem of statecraft must be preceded by this question: "For what purpose does the State exist?" To advance the well-being of its citizens? Which suggests the further question, "What is well-being?" Although one might split hairs for very long on this subject, we of the Western world have a pretty clear notion of the condition which we try to perpetuate and enlarge by our political effort; ample food and warmth, clothing, decent housing, freedom from disease, the security which enables us to go about our business undisturbed; and bound up with this material prosperity, certain spiritual possessions: a desire to live under our own laws, using our language, expressing ourselves freely in a distinct literature and social life—the thing which we call, generally, nationality.

It is to ensure these things that States exist, and the question which brings us immediately to the fundamental problem of war is this: Is the State in ensuring these things to a large degree brought into necessary conflict with other States? Does it, in securing for its citizens the largest opportunities, do so at the expense of the citizens of other States, either negatively or positively—

that is to say, either by keeping them out of possible opportunities, or by turning them out of actual enjoyment of such? If that be true, and if we take the further ground—which I do—that a statesman's first duty is to his own people, then you get what the Greek author two thousand years ago declared was the great tragedy of human life, the conflict of two rights, a condition in which neither party to a difference is able to arrest his action, save at the cost of the betrayal of his trust, though the two actions necessarily converge to collision, and that collision, in the case of States, is expressed in war.

I have given you immediately what I believe to be the best statement of the case for regarding war as an inevitable feature of statecraft in the modern world; a statement, moreover, implying in my view a moral justification to which, it must be confessed, the classic authorities have seemed for the most part to be indifferent.

One need not go back to Machiavelli for a form of statement of this view of the necessary rivalry of nations, the view that nations are "predatory entities," so crude as to sound like the maxims of brigands. You will find Machiavelli's maxims re-stated and re-enforced in the pages of writers like Clausewitz, Steinmetz, de Gartden, Von Ihreing, Bernhardi, in fact, in the pages of most of those who during the last two centuries whether in Germany, France, or England, have dealt with problems of international politics in just such a way. And it is rather a curious fact that those who in recent years have attempted to show these cannibalistic maxims to be, even when judged by the test of interest and advantage, unsound and untenable, are now assailed almost ferociously by certain writers who have, at least in part, supported the older view of statecraft, as applying too sordid a measure to human conduct!

Admiral Mahan, an exponent of orthodox statecraft on its strategical side, criticizes my own work as "a profound misreading of human action," the assumption that nations act from motives of interest being "much less worthy than those which mankind, to do it bare justice, persistently maintains."* This in passing.

I prefer to state the classic statecraft in terms that are capable of moral justification—terms that have been employed by men like Mahan himself in America and Spencer Wilkinson in England; a case based on the premise that statesmen are compelled to do the best possible for their own people, and that, if it is a choice between the interests of our own countrymen and the interests of foreigners, we must choose the interests of our countrymen, just as one does in matters of fiscal policy.

Quite simply and concretely was the orthodox view expressed more than a decade since by the German delegate to the first Hague Peace Conference, Baron Karl von Stengel. This authority lays it down in his book that—

* "Armaments and Arbitration," Harpers.

"Every great Power must employ its efforts towards exercising the largest influence possible, not only in European but in world politics, and this mainly because economic power depends in the last resort on political power, and because the largest participation possible in the trade of the world is a vital question for every nation."

This view has the heartiest endorsement of our own greatest authorities. Admiral Mahan, whose work on the influence of sea power gives him, on his side of the question, an authority second to none, is still more emphatic and still more definite, and in one notable passage* he shows it to be part of his case that the "naval supremacy of Great Britain in European seas means a perpetually latent control of German commerce." The greatest Anglo-Saxon exponent of the old political creed lays it down quite clearly that "the rivalry between Great Britain and Germany is part of the struggle for commercial and industrial predominance which is now going on between the two countries."

In a quite recent book—written the last year—an English exponent of the same view ("Rifleman,") puts the case still more strongly:

"You cannot abolish war from a competitive system of civilization; competition is the root-basis of such a system of civilization, and competition is war. When a business firm crushes a trade-rival from the markets by cut-prices there is exactly the same process at work

* "The Interest of America in International Conditions." Harpers.

as when a business-nation crushes a trade-rival by physical force. The means vary, but the end in view and the ethical principles in question are identical. In both cases, the weaker goes to the wall; in both cases it is woe to the vanquished." ("The Struggle for Bread," p. 209.)

This author adds: "The teaching of all history is that commerce grows under the shadow of armed strength. Every war which we have waged from the days of Cromwell to the present has been to protect British Commerce."* (p. 145).

Surely a similar view is indicated by Lord Roberts when he tells us at Manchester that—

"We have lost command of every sea but one—the North Sea—and our supremacy over that sea is now a matter of dispute. In other words, whereas your forefathers traded as of right on every sea, now you only trade by the sufferance of other Powers."

You can find illustrations of this general principle in any current discussion on the subject. I pitch at hazard, for instance, on an article headed, "Welt Politik," in the current *National Review*, and find the expression of opinion that "Germany *must* expand. Every year an extra million babies are crying out for more room; and as the expansion of Germany by peaceful means seems impossible, Germany can only provide for those babies at the cost of potential foes, and

* I need hardly say I do not share this view. The book from which I am quoting has as sub-title, "A Reply to the Great Illusion."

France is one of them. The same struggle for life and space, which more than a thousand years ago drove one Teutonic wave* after another across the Rhine and the Alps, is now once more a great compelling force. Colonies fit to receive the German surplus population are the greatest need of Germany. This aspect of the case may be all very sad and very wicked, but it is true."

The author adds, aptly enough: "So it is impossible and is absurd to accept the theory of Mr. Norman Angell." And, as a matter of fact, if this author's statement of the case is correct, my theory is absolutely and completely wrong. I will hazard, however, in passing, the guess that the writer of the article in question has not the faintest notion of how that theory is supported; his form of statement implies that it has burked the series of facts to which he refers; whereas, of course, it has been stated in terms of them.

Before giving an abstract analysis of the fal-

* As a matter of simple fact, of course, the "Teutonic waves" were probably never a matter of the pressure of population upon the means of subsistence even in the rudimentary stage of cultivation. Cæsar tells us that the emigrating Germans possessed vast uncultivated lands. ("Commentaries," I., IV., 553.) Gibbon also says: "For my part I have not been able to discover any proof that their (the barbarians') emigration ever proceeded from want of room at home." The modern era of German emigration has ceased (whereas twenty years ago 200,000 Germans left Germany every year practically none leave to-day) now that the population has increased, while the *immigration* into Germany from Russia, for instance, is very large, amounting in 1911 to something like a quarter of a million labourers.

lacy which I believe underlies this notion of the inevitable conflict of States in the pursuit of the object for which they have been created, I will try, by recalling very simple historical facts, to indicate certain processes that have operated in human society, and which give at least a hint of the nature of the fallacy.

When the men of Wessex were fighting with the men of Sussex, far more frequently and bitterly than to-day the men of Germany fight with those of France, or, either, with those of Russia, the separate States which formed this island were struggling with one another for sustenance, just as the tribes which inhabited the North American Continent at the time of our arrival there were struggling with one another for the game and hunting grounds. It was in both cases ultimately a "struggle for bread." At that time, when this island was composed of several separate States, that struggled thus with one another for land and food, it supported with great difficulty anything between one and two million inhabitants, just as the vast spaces now occupied by the United States supported about a hundred thousand, often subject to famine, frequently suffering great shortage of food, able to secure just the barest existence of the simplest kind. To-day, although this island supports anything from twenty to forty times, and North America something like a thousand times, as large a population in much greater comfort, with no period of famine, with the whole population living much more largely and deriving much more from the soil than did the men of the Heptarchy, the "struggle for bread" does not now take the form of struggle between groups of the population.

This simple illustration is at least proof of this, that the struggle for material things did not involve any necessary struggle between the separate groups or States; for those material things are given in infinitely greater abundance when the States cease to struggle. Whatever, therefore, was the origin of those conflicts, that origin was not any inevitable conflict in the exploitation of the earth. If those conflicts were concerned with material things at all, they arose from a mistake about the best means of obtaining them, exploiting the earth, and ceased when those concerned realized the mistake.

So much for the material side. Now for the moral.

Man's most important moral possession is his religion. It concerns his relation not merely to life, but to eternity; and, incidentally, for a very long period in European history, religion was the main pre-occupation of statecraft. The duty of the State to dictate the belief of its subjects was for long a right very tenaciously held; and held on grounds for which there is an immense deal to be said; and it was accepted for long as an axiom, that men were secure in their faith only by virtue of the force they could exercise to protect it, and, that, consequently, so long as men valued their spiritual possessions, military conflicts between the religious groups would be inevitable. This inevitability was a commonplace of discussions on statecraft, especially in France, during the 16th, 17th, and the early part of the 18th centuries. And yet religious wars came to an end, not by virtue of the State imposing peace—the trouble arose largely from just that attempt—but simply because the general development of European thought undermined that conception of the relation of force to religious faith and truth, out of which the conflict arose.

Here we have, then, two very pertinent facts, which bear upon this doctrine of the inevitability of military conflict between groups, whether that conflict be over material or moral questions.

But I want, by the illustration of a further fact, and not yet by abstract analysis, to get a little nearer to the heart of this fallacy of the inevitable conflict of states. The view which I have quoted concerning the necessity of Germany's expansion as a sheer matter of finding bread for her increasing population, has found during the last year or two very general expression. One author declares that in the last resort, Germany's menace is also a struggle for bread; she needs the wheat and food of Canada, or of some other colony, wherewith to feed her children. Well, is it not quite obvious that Germany can have that food now by paying for it, and that even if she conquered Canada, she would still have to pay for it; that the fact of political conquest would make no difference to the problem of subsistence one way or another? I can hint briefly at a process, which I have sketched in very considerable detail elsewhere, in the following passage:

"In the days of the sailing ship and the lumbering wagon dragging slowly over all but impassable roads, for one country to derive any considerable profit from another it had practically to administer it politically. But the compound steam-engine, the railway, the telegraph, have profoundly modified the elements of the whole problem. In the modern world political dominion is playing a more and more effaced rôle as a factor in commerce; the non-political factors have in practice made it all but inoperative. It is the case with every modern nation actually, that the outside territories which it exploits most successfully are precisely those of which it does not 'own' a foot. Even with the most characteristically colonial of all—Great Britain—the greater part of her overseas trade is done with countries which she makes no attempt to 'own,' control, coerce, or dominate; and incidentally she has ceased to do any of those things with her colonies.

"Millions of Germans in Prussia and Westphalia derive profit or make their living out of countries to which their political dominion in no way extends. The modern German exploits South America by remaining at home. Where, forsaking this principle, he attempts to work through political power, he approaches futility. German colonies are colonies *pour rire*. The Government has to bribe Germans to go to them; her trade with them is microscopic;

and if the twenty millions who have been added to Germany's population since the war had to depend on their country's political conquest, they would have had to starve. What feeds them are countries which Germany has never 'owned' and never hopes to 'own'—Brazil, Argentina, the United States, India, Australia, Canada, Russia, France, and England. (Germany, which never spent a mark on its political conquest, to-day draws more tribute from South America than does Spain, which has poured out mountains of treasure and oceans of blood in its conquest.) These are Germany's real colonies."

I have not space here to deal in detail with questions which doubtless occur to you as partially affecting this generalization—the question of hostile tariffs, of preferential treatment for the Motherland and so forth.* All I am trying to do is to suggest to your mind certain facts of the modern world which render the proposition concerning the place of military force as a means to the end for which States exist, as, to say the least, incomplete. Before leaving this particular phase of the question I will hint at certain historical developments in reference to the question of expansion by conquest, which also I have dealt with at greater length elsewhere.

What was the problem confronting the merchant adventurer of the sixteenth century? Here were newly-discovered foreign lands containing, as he

* These points are dealt with in detail in a previous work of mine. *See* "The Great Illusion" (Putnam's), Chapters V., VI., VII., and VIII., Part I.

believed, precious metals and stones and spices, and inhabited by savages or semi-savages. If other traders got those stones, it was quite evident that he could not. His colonial policy, therefore, had to be directed to two ends: first, such political effective occupation of the country that he could keep the savage or semi-savage population in check, so that he could exploit the territory for its wealth; and, secondly, exclusion of other nations from this wealth in precious metals, spices, etc., since, if they obtained it, he could not.

That is the story of the French and Dutch in India, of the Spanish in South America. But as soon as there grew up in those countries an organized community living in the country itself, the whole problem changed. The colonies, then, have a value to the mother-country, mainly as a market, and a source of food and raw material; and if their value in those respects is to be developed to the full, they inevitably become self-governing communities in greater or less degree, and the mother-country exploits them exactly as she exploits any other community with which she may be in relation. Germany might acquire Canada, but it could no longer ever be a question of her taking Canada's wealth in precious metals or of any other form to the exclusion of other nations. Could Germany "own" Canada, she would have to "own" it in the same way that we do; the Germans would have to pay for every sack of wheat and every pound of beef that they might buy, just as though Canada "belonged" to Great Britain or to anybody else. Germany could not have even the meagre satisfaction of Germanizing these great communities, for one knows that they are far too firmly "set." Their language, law, morals, would have to be, after German conquest, what they are now. Germany would find that the German Canada was pretty much the Canada that it is now—a country where Germans are free to go and do go, which is now a field for Germany's expanding population.

Having *illustrated* the difference between the generally accepted theory of the rôle of political power and the facts, I will now attempt to define it in precise terms. The divergence arises primarily from a misconception of the real functions of government in the modern world. The current conception is based upon the image of a State as the economic executive of its citizens, as a limited liability company—or its board—is the economic executive of its shareholders, and a church is the spiritual executive of its members in the matter of dogma or discipline.

And I am afraid this confusion is not merely a "vulgar error." No less a person than Admiral Mahan assures us that the struggle for territory between nations is justified economically, by the fact that just as a steel trust has an advantage in owning its own ore fields, its stores of raw material, so a country has an advantage in owning colonies and conquered provinces. We see at once the idea: the nation is a commercial corporation like a steel trust.

Well, of course, a moment's reflection shows us that the analogy is an absolutely false one; that these pictures of nations as rival units competing one against the other bear no sort of resemblance to the facts.

To begin with, the nations, except in so far as the carrying of letters, and, in some cases, the manufacture of matches and tobacco are concerned, are not commercial corporations at all, but political and administrative ones, with functions of a like kind to those possessed by our villages, towns, or counties, and Germany no more competes with Britain than Birmingham does with Sheffield. It is not the State which owns and exploits the ore fields or farms, or factories, in the way that the Steel Trust owns its sources of raw material. The State merely polices and guarantees possession to the real owners, the shareholders, who may be foreigners. The mere fact that the area of political administration would be enlarged or contracted by the process which we call conquest, has little more direct bearing upon such economic questions as the ownership of raw material by the populations concerned, than would the enlargement of a town's area by the inclusion of outlying suburbs have upon the trading of the citizens of such towns. It is, of course, conceivable that they, or some, might incidentally gain, or incidentally lose, but an increase of wealth is no necessary consequence of the increase of municipal territory, or else it would be true to say: "The people of Toulouse are of course wealthier than the people of Tours," or those of Birmingham than those of Nottingham. We know, of course, that we cannot determine the wealth of a person by the size of the town in which he lives. The largeness of the administrative area may be incidentally a distinct economic disadvantage, as much in the case of a city as in the case of a country.

But the foregoing is only one small part of the fallacy of approximating a nation to a commercial firm. Not merely is it untrue to represent the nation as carrying on trade against other nations, untrue to represent the State as a corporation carrying on the trade of its people, but it is just as untrue to represent the nations as economic units in the field of international trade. We talk and think of "German trade" as competing in the world with "British trade," and we have in our mind that what is the gain of Germany is the loss of Britain, or *vice versa*. It is absolutely untrue. There is no such conflict—no such thing as "British" trade or "German" trade in this sense. An iron master in Birmingham may have his trade taken away by the competition of an iron master in Essen, just as he may have it taken away by one in Glasgow or Belfast, or Pittsburg, but in the present condition of the division of labour in the world, it would be about as true to speak of Britain suffering by the competition of Germany, as it would be to talk of light-haired people suffering by the competition of the dark-haired people, or of the fact that those who live in houses with even numbers are being driven out of business by those who live in odd-numbered houses. Such delimitations do not mark the economic delimitations; the economic function cuts athwart them; the frontiers of the two do not coincide.

When we talk of "German" trade in the international field, what do we mean? Here is the iron master in Essen making locomotives for a light railway in an Argentine province (the capital for which has been subscribed in Paris)—which has become necessary because of the export of wool to Bradford, where the trade has developed owing to sales in the United States, due to high prices produced by the destruction of sheep runs, owing to the agricultural development of the West. But for the money found in Paris (due perhaps, to good crops in wine and olives, sold mainly in London and New York), and the wool needed by the Bradford manufacturer (who has found a market for blankets among miners in Montana, who are smelting copper for a cable to China, which is needed because the encouragement given to education by the Chinese Republic has caused Chinese newspapers to print cable news from Europe)—but for such factors as these, and a whole chain of equally interdependent ones throughout the world, the iron master in Essen would not have been able to sell his locomotives. How, therefore, can you describe it as part of the trade of "Germany" which is in competition with the trade of "Britain" or "France" or "America?" But for the British, French, and American trade, it could not have existed at all. You may say that if the Essen iron master could have been prevented from selling his locomotives the trade would have gone to a British one. But, this community of German workmen, called into existence by the Argentine trade, maintains by its consumption of coffee a plantation in Brazil, which buys its machinery in Sheffield. The destruction, therefore, of the Essen trade, while it might have given business to the British locomotive maker, would have taken it from, say, a British agricultural implement maker. The economic interests involved sort themselves, irrespective of the national groupings.

The notion that it is the nations, and not the trades, which are the rival economic units, can be put to a very simple test—the test of progression. "Great Britain" (adopting for the moment the ruling classification) has admittedly the greatest interest in foreign trade, and it is she who is supposed to be feeling most keenly the competition of rivals. Now suppose that by some magic she could annihilate all these rivals—Germany, the United States, Austria, France, all of them—sink them beneath the sea—would Great Britain be the richer? She would be faced not merely by bankruptcy, but by the starvation of millions of her population; something like a third of it would actually die for want of food, or leave the country.

What, of course, we fail to realize in this connection is that trade is necessarily exchange; if we are to sell anything to anyone the buyer must have money. He can only obtain that money by selling something. If we do not sell we cannot buy; and so when you come to the complex groups embracing all sorts of trades and industries which our modern nations represent, each must, in order to be a customer, be also a competitor. Roughly, and largely in the European nations, he is a customer to the extent that he is a competitor. It is a noteworthy fact, the full significance of which I have not space to deal with now, that it is occasionally those nations which most resemble one another in their industrial make up that are mutually the best customers. Great Britain sells more per head of population to Belgium, a highly industrialized nation, than to Canada or Russia, mainly agricultural nations.

What, however, I am dealing with here is not an ignorance of certain statistical facts, or a failure to understand certain obscure points in economics; not the use of mere loose language, but a fundamentally untrue conception, a false picture of the State in its relation to the economic activities of its people.

Let me summarize the general principles at which we have arrived. Moral conflicts, like the religious wars, arise necessarily from a certain conception of the relations of force to religious facts; a certain conception as to what force could do in the way of protecting religious truth from error or compelling the acceptance of religious truth. As soon as it was realized that this relationship had been misconceived, that force could neither protect nor impose truth, physical conflict in the domain of spiritual affairs came to an end.

So with military conflict concerning material things—food, wealth, prosperity. It arises from a quite definite conception of the relation of military force to those things, the belief that military force can ensure or promote them. When it is realized that military force is ineffective or irrelevant to these ends, its employment as a means thereto will cease, as it has already ceased in the sphere of spiritual things.

I think I hear you say one word: "Police." Well, what is the rôle of the police; how does it differ from that of an army?

What the rôle of the police here in London is we know perfectly well: it is to prevent one citizen using force against another, to run in burglars, and so forth. So doing, it is, properly speaking, a police force. It would become an army if it were to march against another police force, that of Birmingham or Liverpool. Police forces are not used one against the other—armies are.

Now, I quite admit that armies are often used as a police force for the maintenance of order. Our army is so used in India, and is doing by that means, I believe, a work invaluable to civilization. But that is not the problem of a European war. Germany does not need to maintain order in Great Britain, we do not need to maintain order in Germany; the impending or threatened conflict between these two countries has nothing whatever to do with the problem of policing.

If, then, this political conflict between nations is merely due to a misconception, analogous to that which produced the conflict between opposing religious groups, what *is* the place of military force in statecraft?

More and more surely are statesmen coming to realize that its employment for positive ends—promotion of well-being as against other States—is ineffective. The German school, of which General von Bernhardi is, I believe, a fair type, is a declining school, and recent events seem to indicate surely that no European Government is bent upon aggression. But it is impossible to forecast what influences may direct the action of the Governments—some unforeseen turn of events may render one aggressive—and military force is used to-day for the negative purpose of making it impossible for force to be used against us. Armies have just one use as between civilized nations: to prevent their being used. The military force of one State is destined to nullify that of another State, and so reduce both to paralysis. The work of the good soldier, like the work of the good doctor, tends to abolish his own job.

But I hope you will note the reservation that I make—as between *civilized* nations. In another sphere I believe there will long be employment for the soldier—in the sort of work that we have done in India and in Egypt. This is police work, properly speaking, and most of the military force of the world will, perhaps, at no very distant date, be transformed slowly into police force. If Europe, a generation or two since, had recognized the truth of this general proposition, that military power can only be positively useful in the maintenance of order, I think that the chief Powers of Europe would before this have composed their differences and made common cause against certain evils which threaten them all alike. Had we seen more of the truth at which I am driving, our policy with reference to Russia, for instance, might have taken the turn seventy years ago which it is now taking, and by so doing might have avoided a war fought to maintain the integrity of Turkey, have given us a larger place in the councils of the world, and perhaps prevented over large areas of the world's surface, a mass of abominable suffering which does not reflect, I think you will admit, very flatteringly upon European statecraft.

I wonder whether you would excuse, in conclusion, a personal word. I am a Pacifist in the sense that I believe men will best carry on their fight against Nature by ceasing bootlessly to fight each other; that man's advance will be marked largely to the degree to which he can close his ranks against the common enemy that is forever trying to destroy him. But I beg you to note this, that because I do not believe in force, I do believe in defence—that is to say, I do not believe in allowing the other man's force to settle any matter in dispute; and for this reason I have taken the ground that, in performing this function at least—in preventing force being used—the soldier's work is useful. I have never taken the ground that the difference between myself and those who do not agree with me on this matter is necessarily one of moral conceptions at all. I believe that it is one of intellectual conceptions, and should be stated in intellectual terms. Those of you who may have done me the honour to read my books, know that I have laid very great emphasis on this point, and have also tried to do full justice to all that the soldier's profession has of abnegation, dedication to an unselfish purpose, discipline and duty; and you will know also, that in doing what I can to make known what I believe to be true, I have been prompted, not by indifference to national needs or national security, but by the conviction that the emergence of these truths will add to our national security, and furnish surer means for the satisfaction of our real needs.

I believe that war is what Mr. Bonar Law has called it: the failure of human wisdom; that the employment of force as between civilized men is a mistake. It can be eliminated from human intercourse in two ways: by confronting force on one side with equivalent force on the other, so that neither can be employed. That way is the soldier's way. However costly, burdensome, and dangerous it may be, it may be the necessary price of human imperfection. But there is another way: by the growing realization on the part of those who provoke the use of force, that it is ineffective, a realization that will come of the slow and piecemeal enlargement of understanding on this subject. If that way is ever to play its part in the elimination of political war, as it has already played its part in the elimination of religious war, it will be because those who think they see an error or misconception in the matter, do their best, however feebly and obscurely, to clear it up. That may not be specifically the soldier's work, but it is somebody's work; and I believe that soldiers who respect honest endeavour, even though it may not be in their own field, will not disparage it.

V

"TWO KEELS TO ONE NOT ENOUGH"

(Notes of a Debate at the Cambridge Union.)

EARLY in 1912 the President of the Cambridge Union wrote asking whether I would oppose the following motion to be moved by the President of the Navy League of Great Britain:

"That the safety of the British Empire and its trade depends on an unquestioned British Naval superiority, maintained upon the basis of two keels to one of capital ships against the next strongest European Power, and the full necessary complement of smaller craft."

To the invitation of the President of the Cambridge Union, I replied that I would not oppose the motion as it stood, but would do so if it were made to read as follows:

"That the safety of the British Empire and its trade can only be secured," etc.

The Cambridge *Granta* gives the following summary of the proposer's speech:

"Mr. R. Yerburgh, M.P., President of the Navy League, began by reminding the House that in the past our navy had preserved the liberties of Great Britain against foreign aggression, had won for us our Empire, and had saved Europe from the domination of Napoleon. Since then it had not been used in an aggressive manner; rather it had performed the functions of a police force on the high seas. Our forefathers had left us a great heritage and great responsibilities. The only way in which to preserve our heritage and fulfil our responsibilities was to maintain a large navy; on that depended our Empire, our wealth, and our liberty.

"What standard was required in the navy if it was to fulfil its duties? It must be strong enough to take the offensive defensive. In the earlier part of the nineteenth century the navy was allowed to fall below the requisite strength; but in the 'sixties, spurred by the fear of attack by France, those who were responsible for our naval defences woke up and formulated the two-Power standard. This standard seemed to have been abandoned in recent years, and the motto was that it was never safe to leave the defences of the country to the Government of the day. You must have a standard by which to judge their provisions. Hence Mr. Stead had formulated the two-keels-to-one standard, and the Navy League had adopted it. The arguments in favour of this standard were—first, that it directed attention to our needs in the

North Sea; second, that it strengthened the hands of the peace party in Germany. We had nothing to gain from winning a war—everything to lose by being defeated. There was no danger of aggression on England's part, but grave cause to fear that Germany might offend; witness Bismarck's lack of principle and the action of Germany's ally, Austria, in annexing Bosnia and Herzegovina. Moreover, Germany's foreign policy was dictated by the Emperor and his advisers, not by the people. Hence the need for a strong navy. Two keels to one was not too much, since the day when one Englishman was equal to three foreigners was gone. The honourable gentleman went on to show how many ships this country would have to build in order to maintain the two-keels-to-one standard; at present Great Britain had more than two keels to Germany's one. We should only have a bare margin for safety over Germany and her allies in the future. The expense was no difficulty, for the Dominions oversea would help us to bear the burden."

The following is a report of the speech in opposition to the motion supplemented by my notes at the time:

This is not an easy motion to oppose—anyhow for me to oppose—because I am not a non-resister; I believe that aggression should be, and must be, resisted, and I would vote any sum necessary to that purpose—to the last penny and the last man. And yet I am going to oppose this motion, because as it stands it embodies a pernicious and dangerous doctrine, and I am going to indicate an alternative policy.

My honourable friend on the opposite bench may ask why, if I believe in defence, I oppose a motion which aims at securing it so completely. He would probably urge that you cannot have too much of a good thing.

Well, I should come to such conclusion if I did what this motion does—ignore just half the facts.

Let me tell you how I came to be able to oppose at all. As originally submitted to me, the motion read as follows: "That the safety of the British Empire and its trade depends on an unquestioned British Naval supremacy," etc. Such a motion I might not have been able to oppose; but I altered the motion to read thus: "That the safety of the British Empire and its trade can only be secured by an unquestioned British Naval supremacy," etc., and, frankly, I was a little surprised that the honourable proposer should have accepted this change without protest. Not only did he not protest, but the speech which he has just delivered has not given the faintest indication that he has considered the reasons which prompted me to make the change. For him, presumably, armaments are the last and final and only basis of peace, and other means are not worth serious discussion. The motion itself, the change which I made, the proposer's failure to note that change, the speech which he has just delivered—all alike show that he believes that by armaments and force alone can problems of the relationship of nations be solved. And it is because he believes this, because the motion implies that no other efforts are worth while or could ever succeed, that I oppose it. For not only will armaments alone not solve the problem of international relationship, but we shall never get near to solution, and this Empire will never be really secure, until other means are applied as persistently as in the past we have applied the remedy of force. But, not only does the motion ignore the fact that the only satisfactory solution of a misunderstanding is to understand it, but even as a statement for safety by armaments it ignores one-half of the whole problem.

This problem of defence is a problem which must include two parties and two groups of factors, and the motion just simply and gently ignores one party and one group of factors. The nearest that it approaches to including the two, is its implied admission that our policy must be determined by our rival's policy; but it is sublimely oblivious of the fact that our rival's policy is determined by ours, or, indeed, that it is guided by a like group of motives. In other words, a problem which includes two parties is stated in terms of one.

I think I can make what I mean by that quite clear. Just recently we had it laid down by a Cabinet Minister that "the way to make peace secure is to be so strong that victory over your enemy will be certain." Well, it looks self-evident, does it not? The implication is that if you are as strong as all that, no one will attack you. It is one of those political axioms which we parade with serene dogmatism because it sounds unchallengeable, one of those obvious things which ought to be a guide to sound national policy. Well, let us hope that it will not be so obvious that the Germans will adopt it. Do you really believe that it would really make for peace if they did? You know it would make for war. Yet if this is the best way for a nation to secure peace, are not the Germans to be allowed to adopt the best way? Or is this one of those absolute truths which Providence has reserved for the use of the British nation only? Do you not see immediately that this "axiom" is only possible if applied to one party to the dispute? If you apply it to the two, you are asking that each shall be stronger than the other. But war is a matter of two parties; preparation for war is a matter of two parties, all problems of international politics are matters of two parties; and your principles must be applicable to both if we are to find through them the solution of those problems.

The other day at a meeting I had this question: Does Mr. Angell suggest that we be stronger than our enemies or weaker? And I replied quite truthfully, that the last time I had been asked that question was by Germans in Berlin. I begged my questioner to indicate how he would have had me reply to those Germans.

Of course, we shall make no progress in this matter until we place ourselves in the position of the other man. Perhaps it is too much to ask a President of the Navy League to put himself in the German's place. I suppose it would be a dereliction of patriotism to do so. Well, I am going to risk whatever imputation there may be in the process, and to place myself for a moment in the position of the German, not for the purpose of making a case against the Englishman—it is not a case here of one being in the right and the other in the wrong—but the case that *both* are drifting into conflict through misunderstanding each the position of the other, and both the real nature of the relationship which exists between them.

And, as that German, I shall ask nothing that I should not ask as an Englishman; and I shall claim no right nor privilege I would not just as readily, as a German, accord to Englishmen.

Now, the first note that this German makes, on reading this motion, is that the Englishman is *not* ready thus to accord to the German what the German is ready to accord to the Englishman. The very first thing to be noted is that this motion deprives the German of the right of self-defence which the Englishman himself claims.

What does the British Navy League Catechism say? It says: "How does a navy prevent war?" And the answer is: "By manifest strength, showing all likely enemies that war is unprofitable for them owing to the difficulty which your enemy has in defending himself."

Very good. I, the German, demand the right to make myself sufficiently powerful for it to be dangerous for you to attack me. You—oh! I am not bringing the President into this discussion, I am only sketching a dialogue—You, the Englishman, claim superiority of two to one in armaments. That, my dear Englishman, means that it is *not* dangerous for you to attack me, which, according to your own definition of defence, I ought so to make it. You can make this attack with absolute security. I do not even claim equality of armaments, only the right to build such armaments as will make the result of your aggression doubtful; but you will not even leave me *this* poor security. You demand an armament which will make your aggression a mere naval picnic. You will not leave me even a fighting chance. You insist upon having me absolutely at your mercy. You deny to me what is, according to your own definition, mere self-defence. You insist that it is the bounden duty of your patriots to achieve it, but you deny, when you exact such a superiority as you do, the right of German patriots to a like defence.

Now, how does the Englishman meet this case of the German? He admits that there is not equality here,—an equality of privilege that is, but he says, what is a vital necessity to England is merely a luxury to Germany. But that will not do either. Here is the British Navy League literature claiming that a nation's safety should be dependent, not upon the goodwill of foreigners, but upon its own strength. Again, you deny that right to Germans. Germans must be content to rely upon the goodwill of England. How does the Englishman meet that point? Well, it was met the other day by an English Minister, who said that the British Navy could not threaten the meanest Continental village. Well, the British Navy could, I presume, bombard Bremen and Hamburg, and it can do something much more even than threaten great seaports—it can destroy immense wealth in sea-borne commerce, essential to the livelihood of millions of Germans. But that is not all. Here is the very father of the modern philosophy of sea power, the saint by whom the British big navy people swear, laying down this doctrine:

"More and more Germany needs the assured importation of raw materials, and, where possible, control of regions productive of such materials. More and more she requires assured markets and security as to the importation of food, since less and less comparatively is produced within her own borders by her rapidly increasing population. This all means security at sea. Yet the supremacy of Great Britain in European seas means a perpetually latent control of German commerce. The world has long been accustomed to the idea of a predominant naval power, coupling it with the name of Great Britain, and it has been noted that such power, when achieved, is commonly often associated with commercial and industrial predominance, the struggle for which is now in progress between Great Britain and Germany. Such predominance forces a nation to seek markets, and, where possible, to control them to its own advantage by preponderant force, the ultimate expression of which is possession. From this flow two results: The attempt to possess and the organization of force by which to maintain possession already achieved. This statement is simply a specific formulation of the general necessity stated; it is an inevitable link in the chain of logical sequences: industry, markets, control, navy bases."

Sir, if our own philosophy is right, it is not a luxury for which Germany strives, but a vital matter for her future welfare. Take this very significant fact: The retention of the right of capture of private property at sea is defended by what may be termed the corsair party, on the ground that to threaten the enemy's commerce is the most powerful form of pressure which we can exercise against him; that by means of such an instrument we can make him sue for peace. These arguments are used every day by the Admiral in resisting the movement for the immunity of private property at sea. But if this instrument is as valuable as they allege, it means that foreign nations *are* threatened in a vital matter by our naval force. You can't have it both ways. If in reality a country like Germany has no need of a navy to protect her commerce, if she has no commerce that can be preyed upon by a foreign Power, then our retention of the right of capture is no use as an instrument of pressure. If it really is the means of pressure that the Admirals urge, then the Germans—if they, like us, really are entitled to look for their safety to their own strength and not to the good-will of foreigners—are in duty bound to oppose to our navy some force at least capable of checking its operations, to say nothing of the fact that we have for some years now been talking of the needs for supporting France with an expeditionary force—such a plea is made officially by the National Service League. The way for Germany to meet a British expeditionary force is by a navy.

What is the situation which really faces Germans? It is this: That a preponderance such as that which this motion demands enables Britain to dictate absolutely the world policy of Germany. If Mahan is right, if our own philosophy upon which we base the claim for our sea policy is right, the German sees his national destinies controlled absolutely by a foreign Power. His diplomats cannot bargain on a footing of equality because they know that an overwhelming preponderance of power must rest with their rival. A nation expanding at the rate of a million a year is to allow its destinies to drift into the absolute control, in so far as world-policy is concerned, of another and a rival nation. If Great Britain can claim that the loss of the supremacy of the seas would mean for her quick starvation, Germany can claim, if our philosophy is right, that Great Britain's domination of her policy may mean slow starvation.

I assume, of course, that the proposer of this motion gives Germans credit for qualities as high as our own. Indeed, it is an essential part of his case that they are in no way inferior, that they are a remarkably efficient, alert, resolute, and educated people. If they do not possess these qualities to a high degree, he would certainly not ask that in this matter we should have a superiority in strength of arms of two to one. You do not need such superiority as that against a man who is your inferior.

Now, the fact that we *cannot* assume these people to be our inferiors, that their boldness and resolution is a necessary part of the proposer's case, is a fact it is important to keep in mind.

For in that case, this motion involves two contradictory propositions:

(1) That our building will cause him to give up, because his needs are less than ours—that it is a "luxury" with him. That is one.

(2) That we must have preponderating force, because his imperative needs of expansion, etc., are thrusting him to aggression.

Here is the dilemma, and it is a real one:

Either (1) his need is a real and growing one, in which case he will keep up the fight to the point of exhaustion, and he is not going to be frightened by your threats, and this talk of it being a luxury for him is so much insincerity.

Or (2) his need is not a real one at all, and the whole squabble is a matter of nerves and temper and misunderstanding, in which case the most evident policy is one of discussion and arrangement. You do not deal with an angry man by shaking your fist at him unless he is a very cowardly one indeed, and I think we have agreed that such an analogy cannot, and should not, fit the German people.

On both grounds, therefore—that is to say, whether you regard the presumed aggression of Germany as prompted by real and growing needs, or whether you regard it as merely prompted by national vanity and temper—the policy of an immense disproportion of power of this kind stands condemned. In the first case, if his need is deep-seated, he will hold out in this game of beggar-my-neighbour. And I want to bring just this fact to your notice. All the factors are pushing Germany and Austria into closer co-operation, and we may be faced to-morrow by a German speaking political entity of eighty or ninety million people. And you will note this: the President of the Navy League will not hear of us in these calculations including on our side the ships of potential allies. Two keels to one, therefore, means this: That the burden which is borne by four of your rivals will have to be borne by one Englishman. Do not you see that in that case your back must break first? That Germany can afford to play the waiting game, and that more and more your interest will centre on precipitating the conflict?† And this, in reality,

* An author much quoted by the big navy advocates—Mr. Archibald Hurd—in his book "German Sea Power" (John Murray) has a chapter, "The Economic Base of German Naval Policy." In it he examines the question "whether Germany has the ability and the will to continue her recent policy of naval expansion." The result of the inquiry appears to be as follows. "It cannot be doubted that, if present tendencies remain unchanged, the (German) Empire will, before the end of the century, have become by far the richest country in Europe. Long before that point is reached, Germany will be able without an effort to bear the weight of much heavier armaments than she now carries: It is often said that she cannot maintain both the strongest army and the strongest navy in Europe. . . . Whether or not she can do this depends entirely upon her resources in men, money, and manufacturing power, and in respect of these three taken together she is probably already much more favourably situated than any other European State—that is to say, if we leave colonies out of the question."

† A policy to which military expression is already being given in England as witness the following from the leading article of *The War Office Times and Naval Review*, February, 1913.

"The Press of this country seems to be either blind or stupid in regard to the Machiavellian, the devilish policy of Germany. We, at any rate, decline to consider that Power, as it is so frequently described in the newspapers as 'a great and friendly nation' . .

"If Germany, after due warning, persists in the increase of a navy whose avowed object is to attack Great Britain and Great Britain's trade, the most effective way of settling the matter once and for all would be to blow the German Navy out of the water. Seeing that the Anglophobists, who appear to be in a large majority in, the 'Fatherland,' propose in due course—*i. e.*, when the German Navy is sufficiently developed—to attack and destroy the English fleet, there does not appear to be any partiis what many Germans fear, and what to their minds gives some sort of colour to the invasion stories like those with which Professor Delbrück entertained us last summer.

Therefore, not merely do you deny him the right to defend himself, but you ask him to place his destinies in the hand of a small fleet, and you expect him to yield because you threaten him with building ships. Sir, let us be honest for a moment. If another people, smaller than ourselves, presumed to take charge of our foreign policy and calmly asked that our safety should be a matter of their goodwill, and attempted to enforce their doctrine by an overpowering shipbuilding programme, what should we do? We should build ships. Then why do we expect the Germans to do anything else? You are asking another man to do what you would never do yourself; and, if one does that, one assumes that he is very craven, or that he will fight. We cannot, and do not, assume that this people of sixty-five millions are a craven people. We must be assuming, therefore, that the logical outcome of this policy is conflict. If, therefore, your desire is to avoid conflict, whichever view of the case you take, the wise course is to do now what we should have to do even after a war—to come to some sort of arrangement and some sort

---

cular object—in fact, we do not deem it sound policy, calmly to await Germany's convenience in the matter The plan we suggest would, at any rate, bring matters to a crisis without delay."

of understanding. And by an understanding I do not mean necessarily any formal agreement between the two Governments. I mean something much more efficacious—I mean a general enlightenment of the public opinion in both countries as to the real nature of the supposed conflict between them. That is the real ray of hope in the situation. It is possible that my honourable friend will say that such policy is hopeless, that it has failed. Sir, it has never been attempted. Speaking practically, none of our efforts has gone into this direction at all. All our money and all our energies have gone to one half of the problem only, and none whatever to the other half, and consequently the whole thing has been distorted, and has created what we know as the "European armament problem."

Why do I say that all our energies have gone into one half of the problem? Well, I can illustrate that by the presence of the honourable mover and the existence of the organization that he represents.

During his speech he was at great pains to prove by quotations from my own writings and otherwise that war is the outcome of human passion and human folly in the field of international politics. He might have emphasized with truth, as I have tried to do, the fact, that when we had wars in another field—that of religion—they were equally the outcome of passion, intolerance, and misunderstandings. "You must," he says, "look for the cause and explanation of war in the folly and ignorance of mankind." Well then, of course, you would suppose that to make war less likely, to make ourselves more secure, you should get at the cause by seeing wherein our folly consists, and where are the misconceptions which provoke war. That is the very thing that the honourable mover does not suggest, to which he does *not* urge us to devote our energies, to which he does *not* particularly desire his countrymen to devote their energies; and I am afraid it is true of some of his colleagues that it is the thing to which they particularly desire their countrymen should *not* devote their energies.

Now, the President of the British Navy League is necessarily, in point of intelligence and character and readiness to serve his country, far above the average. I hope you will not think it unseemly if I say that he is quite obviously above the average in this respect, in his desire to do well by his countrymen. Yet what form does he give to the services that he furnishes so readily? That of trying to correct what he tells us is the cause of war—that is to say, trying to induce his countrymen to realize the misconceptions which lie at its base? Not the least in the world. He deems the best service he can render his country is to urge it to add to the instruments of war, notwithstanding his certain knowledge that our rivals will immediately meet that increase, and that consequently by so doing we shall not in the least degree add to our ultimate security, but merely to the danger of explosion.

And what he does, most of the best intentioned of his countrymen do. The Englishman of means and leisure goes into the army or the navy; failing that, and yet desiring to show his patriotism, he joins the Navy League or the National Service League. And the patriotic German does the same thing. That, or the equivalent of these things, is what they have been doing through the centuries with this result: that if we do fight it will be the nine thousandth and something war of history, as little likely to settle anything as the preceding nine thousand odd have done. All our efforts have been directed to war, to the preparation of war. If anything like an equivalent effort had been directed to peace, to the preparation for peace, to the understanding of those things which are needed for it, to the overcoming of those obstacles that stand in the way of it, we should have had peace.

Just make the money comparison, though it is perhaps the least important of all, of the proportion devoted to the two halves of this problem. Civilization spends about two and a half billion dollars a year on preparations for war. It includes not merely the training of millions of men who are the mere beasts of burden of war, but also the training of men of learning, the foundation of institutions for the study of the science of war, the systematization of this science, thoroughly and elaborately. How much do we spend on the systematization of the scientific organization of the world? On the endowment, for instance, of International Law, the economic organization of that World State which we know to be growing up? Why, in all the world, you will not find devoted to such objects the price of the smallest battleship. We get tens of thousands of men of culture and education giving trained attention to war, going out to war. How many are the missionaries and soldiers going out to fight the battle against ignorance in this matter; giving their lives to fight the crimes, and the lying and the silly hatreds that mark misunderstandings in this field; going, if you like, into the foreign wilds, if you believe there is no political ignorance in this matter to clear up in our own country.

You take the ground perhaps, that it is impossible to do anything useful in this field, to change public opinion. You may invoke what has already been invoked, the rebelliousness of human nature and human opinion to any change by argument, persuasion, and discussion.

It is curious, that this doctrine of the impossibility of affecting conduct by argument and discussion is only invoked as against Pacifism. When it is a matter of getting more ships or a larger army, the statesmen, or those who control them, can always manage to create and organize opinion. When Admiral Tirpitz decided that Germany was to have a great navy, he knew that the first thing to do was to create a public opinion, and he promptly created it in a very thoroughgoing and systematic manner. He started the

German Navy League, saw that it was subsidized, inspired patriotic writers, entertained professors, made friends with the newspaper men, had the Krupps buy up a newspaper or two, so that in less than ten years German opinion had formulated its demand for a great navy, and, of course, the Government had to be guided by so definitely expressed a national demand. When orders are slack at Krupps, there is no difficulty in arranging that the French agents of that enterprising firm shall circulate in French newspapers statements as to the impending increase of French armaments, which are promptly reproduced (with a new coat of paint) in the German Press. In England we have not one Navy League, but at least two. When our great soldiers want conscription, they do not wait for public opinion—they make it. Lord Roberts—Earl and Field-Marshal—takes the stump, addresses great popular audiences, is most efficiently stage-managed; and for ten years the organization which he patronizes has been industriously at work, doing what must always be done as a precedent to any new action whatsoever, changing the minds of men to a lesser or greater degree.

Here are these two great unofficial bodies, the British and the German Navy Leagues, and their activities just illustrate the defect which at present stands in the way of progress in this matter—the blindness to one half of the problem, the blind philosophy at the bottom of the whole notion which dictates the relationship of nations. Why are those two Leagues not conferring together for purposes of getting at an understanding of the policy behind armaments? They admit that armaments depend upon policy, that the policy of one is bound up with the policy of another; and yet policy is the one thing that they have never discussed together. Why should there not be a section of intelligence, a section of education, what you will, existing in both of these two great bodies, the whole aim of which would be for each to understand something of the motives which were prompting the action of the other? They could do, since they are untrammelled by governmental and diplomatic restrictions, what Governments are unable to do. They have not done it, of course, because, as I said, both are dominated by a blindness to half the factors of the case.

Do you suppose that if for every year during the seventeen years they have existed, these two bodies had met thus to discuss policy, to discuss the why and wherefore of the armaments at all, we should now be faced by the present condition of this problem?

You will say that it is hopeless for great nations to agree not to use force, the one against the other, that the whole idea is chimerical. Well, I will prove to you not merely that it is not chimerical, but that it has been realized in full in very important and thorny cases; that the greatest security is obtained in replacing armaments by understanding.

Forty or fifty years ago, as you can prove for yourself if you read certain Parliamentary debates of the time, England believed herself threatened by the growth of another Power, a Power which has, in fact, become far greater than Germany, and spends more money on her navy than does Germany. She is able to threaten us at far more points; in fact, she could do us very grievous damage.

The Power to which I refer is, of course, the United States of America. We seem for the moment quite to have overlooked the fact that the United States is the most portentous industrial and political rival Great Britain possesses. Just think: it represents a homogeneous political entity of ninety millions—to-day the greatest and most powerful in the world when we consider the high average of activity and efficiency of the people; to-morrow, perhaps, dominating, by virtue of closer relations with Canada on the north, Mexico on the south, and the control of the Panama Canal, half a hemisphere and populations running into one hundred and fifty millions, with resources immeasurably greater than those at the disposal of any other single Government—a Government with which we have been twice at war in the past, a people comprising elements deeply hostile to ourselves. This incalculable political force is able to harass us at fifty points—navigation through the Panama Canal, the relation of our colonies in the Antilles with the continent, our Eastern trade as it affects the Philippines, trans-continental transit to Australia, to mention only a few. As a matter of fact, the points of contact and of difference with our European rivals are trifling in comparison. Surely all this, as much on the economic as on the political side, constitutes a rival immeasurably more disturbing than any which has troubled our sleep within the last few decades—France, Russia, Germany.

How have we protected ourselves from the aggression of this still greater Power? We have protected ourselves by the only means that will ever give us permanent national safety—a better understanding of the real character of the relationship between nations. Here enlightened opinion gives security. Our greatest colonial possession runs parallel to the borders of the United States of America for three thousand miles, and it is the most striking fact in the illustration of these problems, with which we are dealing, that it is the only international frontier in the world which does not possess a fort, nor as much as a gun. Are we threatened by our defencelessness? The one Power that threatens us least is the United States.

In that connection I should like to recall something that is not generally remembered with reference to the work of Cobden. I am often told that because wars have followed Cobden's death, therefore his work for peace has been useless. Well, here is one fact: At a time when feeling against the Northern States was very considerable in Great Britain, and great difficulties had arisen, a bill had been drafted for fortifying the Canadian frontier with Martello towers and rescinding the Rush-Bagot Treaty, by which neither Power puts battleships on the Great Lakes. When this proposal came up Cobden was ill, but he nevertheless came to London to fight it tooth and nail, and he scotched it. But do you believe that if we *had* put battleships on the Lakes, that if we had built those fortifications along the frontier, that if we had had a great British army in Canada, and that if all this explosive material had been lying around when all such difficult and thorny questions of the *Alabama* claims, the seizure of the Southern Delegates, the Venezuelan imbroglio, arose—do you really believe that there would have been no explosion, if explosive material had been there? Do you really believe that if we had had warships confronting one another or armies confronting one another during the last forty years on the North-American Continent, we should, the year after this, be celebrating the centenary of Anglo-American peace? Do you really believe that if we had had these battleships or these armies we should have been more secure in Canada?[1] You know that we

[1] The *Times* of October 9, 1813, has the following comment concerning the naval engagements on the Great Lakes which had just taken place:

"*We are confirmed in the opinion we have already stated, that our*

should have been less secure and that in all human probability we should have lost Canada. I am aware, of course, that no positive data can be brought, that we are discussing only probabilities, but this we can say: If explosive material is there, it *may* go off—if it is not there it *can't* go off. My policy makes peace certain—the other at least uncertain. You may say that it is because of the similarity of speech and language and origins that we are able thus without armies to keep the peace with our neighbours in North America. That conclusion, which is usually drawn, is precisely the contrary to which the obvious facts point. That similarity of origin has created points of contact. There has never during this hundred years been

---

naval pre-eminence on the Lakes is not yet effectually established. In numbers, indeed, it would seem that we are already superior; for, besides the four American schooners already mentioned as lost, two others have been sent into Niagara as unfit for service, but whilst a hostile squadron braves our flag, whilst it ventures out of port to court a contest, we have not that command of the Lakes which it befits our naval character and concerns our most essential interests to maintain. We say not this as implying any doubt of the ultimate event, or any diffidence in that department of the Government to whose care the necessary arrangements for the attainment of this object are committed; but, having ever anxiously pointed the attention of our readers to the vital importance of this part of the national policy, it becomes our duty to remark that the exertion ought not to be slackened, when it is apparently on the eve of being crowned with the fullest success. *If the Government succeed in establishing, as we have every reason to hope it will establish, the undisputed sovereignty of the British flag on the Mediterraneans of North America, it will deserve a commendation similar to that which it has so universally received for rescuing the European Peninsula from the dominion of the Invader.*"

any question of quarrel between the United States and most of those countries divided from her by speech and common origin; with France, with Germany, with Russia, there have been but trivial differences; all the troubles, all the quarrels, have been with us.[1]

If therefore, an unarmed situation of this character is possible between two such rivals as Great Britain and America, what are the material facts which prevent a similar situation as between Great Britain and Germany? If the two most alert, expansive, and enterprising peoples in the world, the people who between them dominate half the surface of the globe, can fight out their differences on other than the military field, so can the others.

What is possible with America is possible with Germany. If we have settled this problem first along the right lines with America, it is mainly perhaps because we could not do anything else,[2] which has enabled us to realize that the solution we have been bound to accept is the solution which it would have been best to accept even if any other had been possible.

If the problem of our relations with Germany is a bit harder, we have also somewhat more machinery with which we can handle it. Berlin is nearer than New York and the German people are

[1] Incidentally if we are going to celebrate the hundred years of Anglo-American peace next year, why should we not celebrate the thousand years of Anglo-German peace?

[2] See Addendum to this paper.

more educated than the Americans. But we are not using the machinery that we possess.

Sir, what is the real difference between us? It is this: That those who put the motion in its existing form can only see one group of facts; we, who oppose it, can see *two*. They are afflicted with a form of political astigmatism, as a result of which half the field of vision is blotted out. When you get two parties, each afflicted with this curious defect—each half blind, that is—and each carrying very explosive machines, accidents of a very nasty kind are likely to occur.

We say: "The first thing is to correct that astigmatism." Our opponents say: "Oh, don't worry about that. The great thing is to have a machine that will make a bigger explosion than the other fellow's." And it does not seem to distress them at all that in the explosion both are going to be blown to smithereens anyhow.

Sir, this motion makes no provision for correcting that defective vision, and that is why I oppose it. So long as that defect exists, the more explosive each makes his engine, the greater does the danger to each become. It is not the line of safety; it is the line of catastrophe.

[The motion was lost by 203 to 183.]

ADDENDUM

I had occasion to illustrate the point that our abandonment of armament rivalry with America is due not to any absence of occasion for conflict, but rather to the fact that fighting is *obviously* futile, by the following article written at the time of the conflict over the Panama tolls, and which the editor to whom I sent it headed, aptly enough:

WHY NOT FIGHT?

THE PARADOX OF PANAMA

When Germany has—

1. Sent us an ultimatum, as offensive in its form as in its matter, summoning us on pain of instant hostilities to submit the dispute concerning the Siamese boundary to the decision of a committee appointed by the Kaiser.

2. Notified us that the acquisition of real estate by English companies or persons on any part of the coasts of Continental Europe, which could, in the opinion of the German Government, be employed for strategic purposes will be regarded as an "unfriendly act" and a violation of the Hohenzollern doctrine.

3. Through the mouth of the Chancellor announced that the real motive behind the recent

revision of the tariff of the German African colonies is the final annexation of British South Africa.

4. Announced that the crew taken from the British ship recently wrecked in the North Sea will be detained by the German police in order that the German Government may make due inquiry into the negligent methods of the British Board of Trade.

5. And, finally, has notified us that rebellions having broken out among certain Sultanates and Khanates along the route of the Bagdad railway, the German Government has decided to take the respective Khans and Sultans under its protection; to acquire definitely a railroad zone along the whole length of the projected line; to build such line; to fortify its termini, to arrange for the free transport of German goods over the said line, the upkeep of which will be defrayed by the added charges on British goods; and further that as most of these acts are in violation of existing treaties, those treaties are henceforth considered null and void and contrary to the German Constitution; and that such of the foregoing acts as violate in addition to the treaties the comity and civilized intercourse of nations shall be considered as covered by the Hohenzollern doctrine aforesaid, which is hereby so extended as to cover them.

When, I say, Germany has done these things, we shall then at last know what we are going to fight about, and the Anglo-German war would have an infinitely greater justification and cause than most of the wars of history.

Well, a Power greater than Germany, in a position to do us far more grievous damage, with a large navy, has, according to the general British view, done all these things, or the American equivalent for them during the last decade or so (for, of course, the Power in question is the United States).* But we have not gone to war, we shall not go to war, we are not even thinking of war.

And it is *not* because "blood is thicker than water." For when the blood was a good deal thicker, when America really was of English blood which it now is not, we went to war, not once but twice; and, curiously enough we fought side by side with Germans (who have never been our enemies in war but always our allies) *against* Americans. So it is not for that reason that we submit to affronts from America which, if committed by Germany, would make war inevitable.

The reason why we shall not go to war is because war would be ineffective; we could not impose our will by war; America is not only impregnable in so far as military force is concerned, but what is perhaps more important in this connection she is quite *obviously* impregnable. We could, it is true, destroy her navy, bombard her ports, blockade her coasts, and by so doing create a position far more onerous for us than for her. She would be embarrassed, we should starve —Lancashire from lack of cotton, other parts of our population from high prices of food; our finances would be chaotic from the havoc which this state of war would make with the British millions sunk in

* *I.e.*, (1) The Venezuelan Boundary Note of Secretary Olney; (2) the recent Bill for forbidding the purchase by European citizens of any real estate on the Western Hemisphere which could have strategic value; (3) Mr. Champ Clark's pronouncement *re* Canadian reciprocity; (4) the action of the U. S. Government with regard to the *Titanic* disaster; (5) the action of the United States in the Panama affairs.

American investments; while America, a self-contained continent, would be much less seriously hit. She does not depend upon foreign food; the foreign money she has already secured; her foreign trade is but a drop in a bucket compared to her internal trade; she can far better afford to be locked in than we can afford to be locked out. Her navy serves no earthly purpose connected with any vital function of her national life. By bombarding her coast towns we could do some damage (not much as all bombardments prove) to property which is mainly ours, and which in the end our insurance companies would have to pay for. But beyond that—nothing. There we should stick. If we landed armies they would be swallowed up in the very spaces of the continent. Do a little sum in arithmetic: If it took three years and nearly half a million of men to reduce a population of about a hundred thousand, inhabiting a territory which could not support them and having no means of manufacturing arms and ammunition, how long would it take to reduce a population of a hundred millions (something like one thousand times as great) inhabiting a territory perfectly able to support them, possessing perfected means of manufacturing the best arms and ammunition in the world; a population, moreover, which possesses just those frontier qualities which were such a source of strength to the Boers, and which has already beaten us in war, not when they were numerically superior as they are now, but when we outnumbered them as a nation five to one? (I am leaving out for the moment the little element of German hostility, which would alone prevent the simple naval seizure of the canal, even if the other factors did not make that impolitic—creating more trouble than it would remedy—which they do.) Certain military truths which, because they were not quite so obvious (and which, indeed, were not so true as they are to-day) had to be learned by experience—in the case of ourselves in North America, Spain in South America, Napoleon in Russia (and elsewhere), France in Mexico, England in the Transvaal, Russia in Korea, Italy in Tripoli—are now in certain cases altogether too obvious to be ignored, as they have been in the past, to the greater prosperity of the war system.

For what is the moral of this Panama business, this cynical disregard of solemn treaty obligations? We are told that it is the failure of arbitration, the impossibility of imposing it or enforcing its awards, the absurdity of depending upon international good faith. Whereas, of course, the real lesson of these incidents is the failure of war, the war system and all that it implies.

We may go to war for the things that do not matter (we have no difference with Germany and probably could not have anything like as serious a one as those that have arisen with America during the last ten or fifteen years), but when a Great Power takes an attitude calculated to hamper our movements and commerce with half the universe we submit, because war—in the preparation for which the nations have piled up armaments to the skies and given an amount of collective effort in excess of that given to any other object whatsoever—is utterly ineffective as an instrument for enforcing our rights. And we have no other instrument, for the simple reason that we have given no equivalent effort to its creation: the effort so far given to the education of the nations in co-operation and common action, to preparation for international organization, is but as a tea-cup to the Atlantic Ocean compared to the time and energy and wealth and lives given to the equipment of the nations for military conflict. And though these immense efforts give us a ludicrously ineffective instrument, we refuse to believe in any other, because, although we have not bestowed the thousandth part of the effort in perfecting them, they are not immediately and entirely effective!

"America" is not to blame in this matter; the best men and the best newspapers of America are as indignant about this thing as we are; the President has done what he can to deprive the movement of its worst mischief. They realize, indeed, that the country as a whole has no earthly interest in violating its obligations for the purpose of relieving a few shipping companies of some of their business expenses, any more than it would have an interest in taxing itself to relieve the railroad, or express, or furniture-moving companies, of some of theirs. But this movement for treaty repudiation owes its force to, and (on the eve of elections) the politicians truckle to, a spirit and temper and opinion on the part of the great mass (generally, as in this case, reflecting ideas which the few at the top are outgrowing), which is the direct outcome of the common political beliefs of Christendom, which we have done our part to uphold—of the military system which results and the efforts to maintain it. These immense armaments of the nations, involving as they do great sacrifices, are the result in each case of an active propaganda, encouraged by governments, organized by leagues and publicists, which, because it takes the shortest cut to secure the immediate object, is naturally and perhaps excusably one-sided and partial. The soldier is not to be blamed for doing his work; it is the civilian who should be blamed for not adding the proper supplement. For if day by day, you urge that a nation must depend upon its own force and that alone, that nations are rival units struggling for predominance in the world, that the country is in danger from the hostility and success of foreigners—the whole almost inevitably producing a patriotism of the "My country, right or wrong" order—you are not likely to get, in the nations, a public opinion calculated to make them work harmoniously together.

And if you do not believe that this is the spirit and temper upon which the American politicians have their eye, just read the sort of arguments by which the baser sort of American paper and the baser sort of American senator support the Tolls Bill. And part of the result of this advocacy (which practically holds the field) is that although military force is fading more and more, we cannot imagine that any international action will succeed which has not military force behind it! We cannot see that civilization has other methods of enforcing its will and bringing a recalcitrant member to book; and if we could see it, we could not avail ourselves of such means since we cannot act together: the temper we have created unfits us for action as a community. You cannot organize so much as a pirate crew until the members have agreed to drop the use of force, the one as against the other. If they continue to fight among themselves, they cannot even indulge in piracy. Unless the majority see the advantage of agreeing, acting in some sort of order, no crew will be formed, and the perception of that advantage by the majority is a matter of ideas. The difference between Turkey and England is not a difference of physical force or soil—the Turk is as strong and warlike as we are, and much of his country as good as ours—but a difference of ideas. If you could fill Turkey with Englishmen, or give the Turks English minds, Turkey would be as orderly as Yorkshire. If ever the nations of Christendom are to become communities—able, like communities of persons, to keep their unruly members in order—you must first get some realization, on the part of each, of the advantage of co-operation. The basic fact of the whole matter is certain ideas concerning the nature of the relations of one State to another; and until you get some modification of those ideas, arbitration will be mainly a pious aspiration. And when you have got that modification of those ideas, arbitration will not be necessary (or necessary with infinite rarity) any more than it is necessary between England and Australia, which communities, like England and America, have realized that the use of military force is unavailing. And that is the outstanding fact: whether we have the wisdom to create a new instrument or not, the old one, however pathetically we may cling to it, has failed. And not only has it failed; it produces the very evil which it was forged to prevent.

VI

CONCERNING THE INTERNATIONAL POLITY MOVEMENT

[EARLY in 1912, a small group of public men in England, desirous of securing for the fundamental principles of foreign policy more scientific consideration than they generally receive, took steps to form a definite organization to encourage such study. As a result of these steps there was formed, owing largely to the generosity of Sir Richard Garton, "The Garton Foundation to Promote the Study of International Polity."

In September, 1913, the first general conference of those taking part in the work of the Foundation and allied bodies or interested therein was held in France, several French and German co-workers being present. The members of the Conference were welcomed in the explanatory address which follows.]

What prompted Sir Richard Garton to found the organization which bears his name? (Incidentally, I should like to make known the fact that it bears his name not as the result of any suggestion from himself, but of one coming unanimously from Lord Esher, Mr. Balfour, and myself.)

Why, if Sir Richard Garton had desired to

promote the idea of agreement between nations and the cause of international order, did he create another organization, when there were hundreds of Peace Societies already in existence, conducted by earnest, disinterested and capable men? You may say, perhaps, that these societies had not emphasized the economic side of our doctrine. Surely, however, it would have been easy to induce them to do so. The economic argument for peace is not a new one; its case was stated long ago with incomparable lucidity by Cobden, and he has had worthy successors to carry on the tradition in our generation in men like Francis W. Hirst of the *Economist*.

Unless we who are identified with this newer movement and the organizations in which it is embodied can make this point clear, I do not think that we shall have shown any *raison d'être* at all, because both the moral and the economic arguments for peace were already being ably urged by existing organizations.

Perhaps I can make our position clear by a trivial illustration. Here is our friend Thomas who was greatly wronged years ago by his friend Jones, who after this particular act of treachery disappeared. Ever since, Thomas has declared that if Jones should reappear he would kill him. One day he learns that Jones *has* returned and is living in the same town. Immediately the friends of Thomas, in order to avert the threatened tragedy, try to dissuade him from his long-declared intention. One group make strongly the moral and religious appeal, endeavouring to bring home to the would-be murderer all that he should remember on that side. Another group confines itself to pointing out the inevitable consequences here in this world of the act he contemplates, the distress and poverty which will ensue to his family, and so forth. But neither the one argument nor the other seems likely to check the blazing passion of murder that burns in Thomas's heart, and both groups of friends feel themselves faced with probable failure. There then appears upon the scene a third party who says: "It will perhaps serve some purpose to point out to Thomas that the man who has turned up is not the Jones who wronged him at all, but quite another and harmless person. Jones, his enemy, died years ago."

It is, I think, quite evident, that if this third party can prove their case, theirs is likely to be the most effective appeal, and that from the moment Thomas really realizes that this other Jones is not *the* Jones at all and that his enemy is dead, his passion will disappear. It is true that you will not have turned him from his deed by any appeal to his higher nature, or to his lower either for that matter; you will simply have pitched upon what is in the circumstances, the most relevant fact to bring to his notice.

Now I think that we of the Garton Foundation, in the facts which we are trying to bring to the attention of the public, do represent to some extent that third party. We attempt to show the *irrelevance* of war to the ends either moral or material for which States exist. This irrelevance has never perhaps been clearly demonstrable until our day. The facts on which the demonstration mainly reposes are facts in large part peculiar to our generation. I do not think that the facts showing the waste or wickedness of war *are* peculiar to our generation. Perhaps the wickedness of war could have been brought more vividly to the mind of the mass of men a century or two since than nowadays. Indeed, if there can be degrees in such a matter, war is less wicked, perhaps now than it was; the suffering is less, the mortality is less, the outrages are less (I am talking of war by the Great Powers), and it is not of such long duration. Nor is it true that, relatively to our wealth, it is more costly than it used to be; the devastation of warfare in the past quite frequently cut a population in half through sheer starvation. War is less, not more devastating, than it used to be. I am not sure even that it disturbs the affairs of the world as much as it used to; indeed it is pretty certain that it does not, although its effect, such as it is, is felt over a much wider area. *The one great thing that modern conditions have done is to enable us to say that war is irrelevant to the end it has in view.*

I will put it in another way. Both of the first two parties of Thomas's friends assumed it as true without query that the Jones in question was *the* Jones; their premises were the same as his own.

Now, even admitting the premises, there was a great deal they could tell Thomas to dissuade him from his act. What they were saying as to its wickedness, its material results to himself, was perfectly true and a strong case against committing it could be made out. And because that was a strong case and because there was a great deal to be said, even assuming the premises true, they have been stating that case and saying those things—and leaving the premises unchallenged. Their pleas might have been successful and might be sufficient, especially if he had considerable religious and moral feelings, or was cautious. But if he were a headstrong and violent man, subject to fits of passion, apt to talk of his honour, apt to think at the back of his mind, in his pagan way, that it was a fine thing to slay the man who had grievously wronged you—why, the chances are that his passion would break through. But if you could change the fundamental assumption on which his feelings and his arguments alike were based and show him that it was all a case of mistaken identity, you would almost certainly turn him from his course. Very decent and humane fellows will wreak vengeance at times on those who have wronged them; only men debased to the plane of insanity feel any satisfaction in punishing harmless, inoffensive Smith for something Jones has done. And the bulk of mankind is not debased to that plane, or our civilization, even such as it is, could not exist.

Now the old Pacifism, in large part, accepted the

premises on which the warrior based his case. I admit that even in doing so there was a great deal to be said against that case, and the Pacifist has been saying it; but the foundations of the military creed have remained unshaken. Now, I think I can make that plain by very recent events.

We in England have just passed through a typical period of friction. I refer to the Anglo-German situation. That period, with all the incidents that marked it, is a good type of what we and most European countries go through from time to time; it is a period of ill-feeling, suspicion, enormously increased armaments, and danger of war.

Now, there is no mystery as to why the panic or ill-feeling or hysteria, or whatever you like to call it, arises. You can trace its growth quite easily; and what is true of the Anglo-German situation is true of the Franco-German, the Russo-German, or of the past Anglo-Russian and Anglo-French cases.

First there comes the allegation that we are insufficiently protected against some alleged hostile intentions—for if you can't allege the hostile intention, you can't make out your case for insufficient protection. The problem of what is adequate defence depends necessarily upon the force which is to be brought against you; and if there is no hostile intention, nor likelihood of it, obviously you are not in danger. So first you get the aforesaid statement of a hostile intention—of the march of Russia upon India, or the projected invasion by the French Emperor, or the determination of Germany to challenge our existence. In the Anglo-German case you had a writer of repute like Mr. Frederic Harrison, or a very popular one like Mr. Blatchford, declaring that it is Germany's intention to destroy us, followed, it may be, by a great public man like Lord Roberts, who tells us with no sort of reservation that Germany will strike when she is ready. You then get, from a Cabinet Minister it may be, a statement of our dangerous situation.

Now, how have Pacifists met these two points of the present case—that Germany is going to attack us and that we are insufficiently protected? They have met them, first, by saying that Germany had no intention of attacking us, and, secondly, that we were sufficiently protected. And I say that in doing so we do not get at the root of the matter at all.

Assume for the sake of argument that you speak with some knowledge of German conditions, and that you tell your countrymen that there exists no serious concerted hostile intent against them on the part of Germany. The unconvinced Englishman will probably ask: "Then why do the Germans go on increasing their fleet?" And then you give the reasons which justify Germany's possession of a fleet quite apart from any intention to attack England. And then your industrious disputant is apt to rejoin: "All that may be true, but what proofs have you? You may be mistaken, and we must provide against that possibility."

Now as a matter of fact you cannot give him any proofs concerning Germany's intention; no man on earth can; because no man can say what a nation of sixty-five or forty-five million people will do five, ten, or fifteen years hence. You cannot tell what your own country will be doing five years hence in so relatively simple a matter as Woman's Suffrage or the Irish question, whether indeed, the British Government will be Liberal or Conservative, or Socialist or Suffragist. How is it possible to give any assurance therefore concerning the action of a whole people five or ten years hence in the complex field of foreign politics?

"Well," will conclude your British questioner, "as it is impossible to say what the future may bring forth, the safest course is to provide for the worst, and, in so vital a matter as naval security, do so by maintaining unquestioned superiority."

And, of course, the Germans are perfectly entitled to reason in a similar way and to adopt an analogous policy, and that lands us straight into a period of armament competition, with all the cost, ill-feeling, misunderstanding, and danger that it involves.

So much for the first point. As to the second, when the Pacifist attempts to show that we are sufficiently protected, he is on still more slippery ground. There is no such thing as adequate protection by armaments—a dictum that would strike us immediately as obvious if we were accustomed to think of war, necessarily a problem of two parties, in terms of two parties, instead of in terms of one. I will show you what I mean.

Mr. Churchill lays it down as an axiom that the way to be sure of peace is to be so much stronger than your enemy that he dare not attack you. One wonders if the Germans will take his advice. It amounts to this: Here are two men likely to quarrel; how shall they keep the peace? Let each be stronger than the other, and all will be well. This "axiom" is, of course, a physical absurdity. On this basis there is no such thing as adequate defence for either. If one party to the dispute is safe, the other is not, and is entitled to try and make itself so.

So you see the line taken, simply of denying that Germany has this intention of aggression, is inefficient; you cannot give any data, while your opponent gives a good deal of data—of sorts.

Those who, with Lord Roberts, urge the likelihood of aggressive action on the part of Germany, point to Germany's expanding population, her need for colonies, for sources of raw material, her desire to extend the German heritage of speech and tradition, and so on; they contend that, having the power, she could starve us into submission as a means to those ends; and that consequently we have to provide against these terrible contingencies.

Just before sitting down to write these lines, I opened by accident the current *National Review* and in an article on "Welt Politik" occur these lines:

"Germany *must* expand. Every year an extra million babies are crying out for more room, and as the expansion of Germany by peaceful means seems impossible, Germany can only provide for those babies at the cost of potential foes, and France is one of them.

"A vanquished France might give Germany all she wants. The immense colonial possessions of France present a tantalizing and provoking temptation to German cupidity, which, it cannot be too often repeated, is not mere envious greed but stern necessity. The same struggle for life and space which more than a thousand years ago drove one Teutonic wave after another across the Rhine and the Alps is now once more a great compelling force. Colonies fit to receive the German surplus population are the greatest need of Germany. This aspect of the case may be all very sad and very wicked, but it is true. . . . Herein lies the temptation and the danger. Herein, too, lies the ceaseless and ruinous struggle of armaments, and herein for France lies the dire necessity of linking her foreign policy with that of powerful allies."

Now, if the underlying assumption of the relation of military power to expansion is correct—if it is for Germany a choice between hardship for her children, permanent exclusion from the good things of the world, and military expansion—then the National Reviewer, and Lord Roberts and Mr. Churchill and Mr. Borden and Mr. Blatchford and Mr. Frederic Harrison are absolutely right. There is a real conflict of interest between these two groups, and force alone can settle it; and on the side of the war party will be invoked not merely base and sordid motives, but some of the noblest as well as the most elemental that guide men's conduct—the determination that their children shall not starve, that they will discharge their obligations to those dependent upon them, and the feeling that those who at present possess the great spaces of the earth, have, since they took them by force in the past, no exclusive right to them, and that others are entitled to assert their right by force if they can.

Pacifists who resist these arguments base their case mainly on the fact that a country like Germany is too civilized to advance by those means, or that she would be too cautious; that she would not take the risks involved in such a method of expansion; that it would be too expensive, would disturb too much her credit and trade; that she cannot find the money—a view for which, as I have admitted, there is an immense deal to be urged, just as the friends of Thomas found a great deal to say on the grounds of morality and interest in trying to persuade him not to slay Jones. But such arguments cannot be conclusive. Given great need, all cost is relative.

Each fears the other may be impelled by need to commit an aggression, or to use force to the disadvantage of the weaker Power. Each believes the other would have an interest in so doing.

Such assumption is quite clearly indicated in the current discussions of the subject. On the British side we have quite recently had several notable expressions of opinion which indicate very clearly what I am trying to enforce. Mr. Winston Churchill, the First Lord of the Admiralty, in his justification of preponderant naval power, declared that "the whole fortune of our race, treasure accumulated during so many centuries, would be swept utterly away if our naval supremacy were impaired"; Mr. Borden, the Canadian Prime Minister, has declared that, "even without war, the mere possession of stronger power by a rival nation would take from us the sole guarantee of the nation's continued existence, and that the loss of a single battle would practically destroy the United Kingdom and shatter the British Empire."

Mr. Frederic Harrison wrote the other day that a naval defeat would mean for England bankruptcy, starvation, chaos.

But if foreign nations want to bring about these things, it is surely because they hope to secure advantage by so doing. If "the destruction of the British Empire," whatever that may mean, is going to do harm to our rival, he will not try to bring it about; and Lord Roberts hints more clearly at the thought that is in the mind of all these statesmen when he says, as he did at Manchester the other day, that Great Britain would carry on her trade on the mere sufferance of any foreign nation that had greater naval power. What he evidently had in his mind was that a stronger power could *transfer* our trade to itself. If there is a danger of foreign nations attempting to break up *our* Empire and trade as the British Statesmen suggest, it is because they assume that the Empire stands in the way of *their* expansion and trade.

Now the whole point of my indictment of most Pacifist propaganda is this: that it has not in the past clearly and simply challenged these fundamental assumptions; nor does it do so to-day. It does not consistently urge and make plain to the common mind that the whole dispute about military power and conquest is irrelevant to these needs of the German people; that if the matter is in reality, as alleged, a "struggle for bread," if Germany needs the wheat of Canada wherewith to feed her people, she can have it now by paying for it, and would still have to pay for it if she "conquered" Canada; that military force has nothing to do with the problem on the one side or the other; that military conquest could not secure food for Germany's expanding population, could not help her expansion, nor even extend the area of her speech and social institutions; that if, for instance, "the Prussian ideal" is to be imposed on Europe, the greatest problem of its advocates is to overcome its enemies in Germany, and not abroad; that conversely—to meet the case of Lord Roberts, Mr. Churchill, and Mr. Frederic Harrison—if ever England is to see her trade or colonies transferred to other hands it will not be as the result of naval disasters; that if ever her population are faced with starvation or emigration—which in some circumstances is an arguable proposition—it will not be because trade routes are blockaded by hostile cruisers; that the loss of trade and the possibility of starvation do represent dangers, but that they could be fought by the provision of battleships as little as you could destroy the bacilli of typhoid fever with twelve-inch guns; that in other words, military force has become irrelevant to the struggles, whether material or moral, of civilized nations; and that the effective forces for the accomplishment of the aims which men desire—whether well-being or the achievement of some moral idea—have shifted from the plane of military force to another.

You may ask why I am so dogmatic in asserting that these more fundamental considerations have not been urged. You probably have the impression that public discussion rages a good deal round these points.

Well, you can get quite exact data. This period of strain between England and Germany has been marked by several very much discussed declarations on the part of great public men. I have taken four as a type: Lord Roberts, Mr. Churchill, Mr. Borden (the Canadian Prime Minister), and Mr. Frederic Harrison—I exclude the Maxses and the Garvins and the Blatchfords, although as a matter of fact they are the most important of all. But take Mr. Churchill's:

"The whole fortune of our race and Empire, the whole treasure accumulated during so many centuries of sacrifice and achievement would perish and be swept utterly away if our naval supremacy were to be impaired."

Now Mr. Churchill is a Cabinet Minister, making a declaration of policy of the greatest possible moment. Here, if ever, was an occasion for those of us who believe that the fundamental conception is false to make our voices heard. Well, you may search all the principal newspapers of Great Britain, lay and pacifist, and *you will not find one that even raises the point to which I am calling attention.* If you follow the discussion, you will find it ignores the fundamental question of whether complete victory by Germany will achieve this end, and rages instead round such questions as whether a foreign army could be landed, whether it could operate when once landed with its communications cut, and the possibility of starvation for this country is discussed in terms of battleships and the protection of trade-routes.

Concerning Lord Roberts's declaration, there was one reference to this in the shape of a letter to the *Manchester Guardian* written by my friend Mr. Haycock, and in it he says:

"If you will examine systematically, as I have done, the comments which have appeared in the Liberal Press, either in the form of leading articles, or in letters from readers, concerning Lord Roberts's speech, you will find that though it is variously described as "diabolical," "pernicious," "wicked," "inflammatory," and "criminal," the real fundamental assumptions on which the whole speech is based, and which, if correct, justify it, are by implication admitted; at any rate, in not one single case that I can discover are they seriously challenged.

"Now, when you consider this, it is the most serious fact of the whole incident—far more disquieting in reality than the facts of the speech itself, especially when we remember that Lord Roberts did but adopt and adapt the arguments already used with more sensationalism and less courtesy by Mr. Winston Churchill himself.

. . . "During the last eighteen months I have addressed not scores but many hundreds of meetings on the subject of the very proposition on which Lord Roberts's speech is based and which I have indicated at the beginning of this letter; I have answered not hundreds but thousands of questions arising out of it. And I think that gives me a somewhat special understanding of the mind of the man in the street. The reason he is subject to panic, and "sees red," and will often accept blindly counsels like those of Lord Roberts, is that he holds as axioms these primary assumptions to which I have referred—namely, that he carries on his daily life by virtue of military force, and that the means of carrying it on will be taken from him by the first stronger Power that rises in the world, and that that Power will be pushed to do it by the advantage of such seizure. And these axioms he never finds challenged even by his Liberal guides.

The issue for those who really desire a better condition is clear. So long as by their silence, or by their indifference to the discussion of the fundamental facts of this problem, they create the impression that Mr. Churchill's axioms are unchallengeable, the panic-mongers will have it all their own way, and our action will be a stimulus to similar action in Germany, and that action will again re-act on ours, and so on *ad infinitum*.

"Why is not some concerted effort made to create in both countries the necessary public opinion, by encouraging the study and discussion of the elements of the case?"

So far as I could find out, there was in the discussion which marked these pronouncements of Mr. Churchill, Lord Roberts, and the rest, no one single pacifist protest against the premises on which they are based. One can only assume that Pacifists accept them. I do not imply that either individuals or organizations have ignored the speeches and statements; there have been formal and lengthy protests in great number. All that I urge is that the one consideration which is most relevant to the whole problem has been ignored.

Well, that is why the Garton Foundation has been established: to direct attention to the most relevant point. And I want to say parenthetically but with all the emphasis of which I am capable, that agreement upon the desirability of doing that does not and need not imply agreement as to the best course with reference to the present armament problem. I come back to my illustration of Thomas and Jones. So long as Thomas *thinks* that Jones is *the* Jones the latter is in danger quite as much as though he really had committed the crime. His policy is evident: to do his best to make it plain to Thomas that there is a case of mistaken identity, and to protect himself meanwhile. Opinions as to the best means of doing that may vary in infinite degree. Some may think it best for Jones to try and frighten Thomas—to shake his fist in his face. Others may think, given Thomas's character, that this is quite wrong and that he is never likely to be frightened. But, however we may differ as to the best defensive means, we can all, if we admit that there is a mistake of identity, agree that it is desirable to convince Thomas of that fact.

I want particularly to emphasise this point in order to show that the educative policy of the Garton Foundation is one which can equally be supported and approved by the soldier, the Navy League man, the Universal Military Service man, or the naval economist and the Quaker.

There are one or two points that I would like to deal with.

You may say first that this irrelevance of political dominion and conquest to industrial and commercial ends of which I have spoken has for years found at least tentative expression by the Manchester School and by Continental economists and Pacifists—Passy, Ives Guyot, de Molinari, d'Estournelles de Constant, Novikow; secondly, that to imply that political power has no bearing on these ends, to challenge absolutely the whole premises, is to enunciate a proposition that is untenable; that it is too sweeping; that its data is too complex for popular treatment, and that to crystallize it in the way I have hinted would be to tie the opposition to war to a thesis which criticism might prove to be in its complete form unsound. I want to answer these two objections.

It is quite true that the ideas we are discussing were outlined and forecast by the men whose names I have mentioned, and I wish I could find fit expression to emphasize our sense of debt to them. There is not, and never has been, on the part of those of us whose efforts centre round the Garton Foundation, any intention or desire to belittle the value of their work. But we recognize this: that the history of all ideas destined to affect human conduct is marked by two fairly well-defined stages—the first in which the ideas are nursed by a somewhat limited academic discussion, and the second when they begin to receive application to policy. The ideas associated with Cobden's name were a commonplace of academic discussion seventy years before he began to apply them to actual policy. Montaigne was laughing at witchcraft two hundred years, and most educated men agreed with him a hundred years before the last execution for witchcraft. Hero of Alexandria, two centuries before Christ, describes several methods of applying steam to power; the Marquis of Worcester possessed a working steam-engine a hundred years before Watt patented his; Newcomen's engine pumped water and worked for nearly a century before the principle which was thus being used had seriously affected English industry. The phenomenon could be illustrated to infinity. Certain collateral conditions are needed before any idea is capable of practical application.

However long these ideas of ours may have been a commonplace of the academic discussion of Pacifism and abstract economics, there have, until our time, been wanting certain simple mechanical facts likely to bring home the truth to the million (which alone can make them part of practical politics)—such facts as the elaboration and extension of a world-wide credit system, which has created a condition of interdependence between the nations never before known. This doctrine could not, originally, affect policy, because its truth could not be made visible.

We are now in possession of facts which do enable us to crystallize into a definite and comprehensive social and political doctrine, of a quite simple nature, likely to affect public opinion, the principle of the futility of military force as applied to the things for which the world is striving. We are able to show how and why the transfer of wealth or trade or moral possessions or ideals (for the same process which makes the material object impossible also makes the moral) cannot be achieved by military force. We can demonstrate by fact that the mechanism of trade, the processes of wealth-making, do not permit of transference in this way; and that this is the result, not of any mere accident—just because it happens—but because human society is so shaping itself, and necessarily so shaping itself, as enormously to increase the element of mutual dependence the one upon the other. That element has increased not merely in degree, but in extent and area; it is not simply that, if the mythical German invader were to sack the Bank of England, the German merchant would pay the piper perhaps equally with ourselves, but that other merchants—French, American, Italian—would in some degree suffer also. It is not merely that the prospective rivals are dependent the one upon the other, but that third, fourth, fifth, and sixth parties are equally dependent upon the interdependent situation of the first two.

Thoroughly to appreciate the meaning of this situation is to recast our conceptions not merely of the morality or otherwise of warfare, but of the mechanism of human society, and to recast mainly one fundamental conception, that of the relation of force to social advantage.

It is possible to reduce the thing to a system easily understandable; to furnish a simple social and economic philosophy of trade and the ordinary activities of life; to give the common man a pretty clear and well-defined working hypothesis of a warless civilization. For this is certain · merely to disentangle detached facts, merely to express a general aspiration towards better things, is no good when we are opposed by a system as well-defined and understandable in its motives and methods as is the war system of Europe. To a system like that, reposing upon a quite definite philosophy, upon a process which is intelligible to the ordinary man, you must oppose, if you hope to replace it, another system, another working hypothesis which you must demonstrate to be more in accordance with facts.

I think you will agree that I do the Peace Societies no injustice, that I do even the economic Pacifists no injustice, as it certainly is no reflection upon them in any way, if I say that their efforts at education and propaganda did not take the form of showing clearly this change in the structure of human society, of revealing the process, of showing the how and why of the futility of military force. There are ample reasons perhaps, why the efforts of Peace Societies went for the most part into other directions.

Now as to the other objection I have indicated—that this hypothesis is too sweeping, that it ties Pacifists to a principle liable to many objections.

In this connection I want to draw a parallel. How has war disappeared in the past? How did religious warfare—at times the bloodiest, most hateful, most passionate, most persistent warfare that ever devastated Europe—come to an end? Obviously it has not been the work of Conventions and Treaties between the religious groups—though that plan was for the best part of a century tried by the statesmen of Europe without success. Nor has it been the result of government "imposing" peace—indeed, the wars largely arose from an attempt to do that.* Obviously it was a matter of advancing opinion, a change of ideas and intellectual conceptions in Europe. The cessation of religious war indicates the greatest outstanding fact in the history of civilized mankind during the last one thousand years, which is this: that all civilized governments have abandoned their claim to dictate the belief of their subjects. For very long that was a right tenaciously held, and it was held on grounds for which there is an immense deal to be said. It was held that, as belief is an integral part of conduct, that as conduct springs from belief, and the purpose of the State is to ensure such conduct as will enable us to go about our business in safety, it was obviously the duty of the State to protect those beliefs, the abandonment of which seemed to undermine the foundations of conduct. I do not believe that this case has ever been completely answered. A great

* "On April 19, 1561, was drafted a pacification edict by which the members of the two factions (Huguenot and Catholic) were prohibited from abusing each other. . . . The Huguenots were permitted to exercise their religion and granted the power to hold synods with the authorization of the Sovereign. Contrary to all the hopes of the Chancellor, the Edict of Toleration was not, however, the first step towards pacification, but towards the wars of religion."—Ruffini, "Religious Liberty."

many believe it to-day, and there are great sections of the European populations and immensely powerful bodies that would reassert it if only they had the opportunity. Men of profound thought and profound learning to-day defend it; and personally I have found it very difficult to make a clear and simple case for the defence of the principle on which every civilized government in the world is to-day founded. How do you account for this—that a principle which I do not believe one man in a million could defend from all objections—has become the dominating rule of civilized government throughout the world?

Well, that once universal policy has been abandoned, not because every argument, or even perhaps most of the arguments, which led to it have been answered, but because the fundamental one has. The conception on which it rested has been shown to be, not in every detail, but in the essential at least, an illusion, a *mis*conception.

The world of religious wars and of the Inquisition was a world which had a quite definite conception of the relation of authority to religious belief and to truth—as that authority was the source of truth; that truth could be, and should be, protected by force; that Catholics who did not resent an insult offered to their faith (like the failure of a Huguenot to salute a passing religious procession) were renegade.

Now what broke down this conception was a growing realization that authority, force, was irrelevant to the issues of truth (a party of heretics triumphed by virtue of some physical accident, as that they occupied a mountain region); that it was ineffective,* and that the essence of truth was something outside the scope of physical conflict. As the realization of this grew, the conflicts declined.

So with conflict between the political groups. They arise from a corresponding conception of the relation of military authority to political ends—those ends for which governments are founded—the protection of life and property, the promotion of well-being. When it is mutually realized by the parties concerned that security of life and property, like the security of truth, is not derived from military force; that military force is as ineffective, as irrelevant, to the end of promoting prosperity as of promoting truth, then political wars will cease, as religious wars have ceased, for the same reason and in the same way.

That way was not by the complete destruction, in the mind of every person concerned, or even in the minds of the majority, of the misconception on which the old policy was based. But the essentials were subconsciously sufficiently in the ascendant.

I want to illustrate how essential truths may emerge almost unconsciously.

*In the preamble to the Edict of Toleration of November 17, 1787, Louis XVI admits the futility of the efforts made by his predecessors to reduce their subjects to unity of faith.

Two hundred and fifty years ago an educated man, with a lawyer's knowledge of the rules of evidence, condemned an old woman to death for changing herself into a cow or a goat. Ask a ten-year-old boy of our time whether he thinks it likely that an old woman would or could change herself into a cow or a goat, and he will almost always promptly reply, "Certainly not." (I have put this many times to the test of experiment.) What enables the unlearned boy to decide right where the learned judge decided wrong? You say it is the "instinct" of the boy. But the instinct of the seventeenth-century boy (like the learning of the seventeenth-century judge) taught him the exact reverse. Something has happened. What is it?

We know, of course, that it is the unconscious application on the part of the boy of the inductive method of reasoning (of which he has never heard and could not define), and the general attitude of mind towards phenomena which comes of that habit. He forms by reasoning correctly (on the prompting of parents, nurses, and teachers) about a few simple facts—which impress him by their visibility and tangibility—a working hypothesis of how things happen in the world, which, while not infallibly applied—while, indeed, often landing the boy into mistakes—is far more trustworthy as a rule than that formed by the learned judge reasoning incorrectly from an immense number of facts.

Such is the simple basis of this very amazing miracle—the great fact which is at the bottom of the whole difference between the modern and mediæval world, between the Western and the Eastern. And it is in some such way that we can bring before the mind of the European public the significance of a few simple, ascertainable, tangible facts in such fashion, that they will frame unconsciously a working hypothesis of international society, which will lead to deductions sufficiently correct and sufficiently widespread to do for the political groups what has already been done for the religious groups.

To impress the significance of just those facts which are the most relevant and essential in this problem, to do what we can to keep them before public attention and to encourage their discussion, is the work of our movement; to discern the best method and to find the means of doing that is the work of this Conference.

INDEX

www.ingramcontent.com/pod-product-compliance
Ingram Content Group UK Ltd.
Pitfield, Milton Keynes, MK11 3LW, UK
UKHW021311181224
3751UKWH00006B/77

9 781019 622544